AWAKE AND READY

How to Work with *Energy* and *Motivate Anyone*

Susan (Usha) Dermond

CRYSTAL CLARITY PUBLISHERS   Commerce, California

CRYSTAL CLARITY PUBLISHERS
1123 Goodrich Blvd. | Commerce, California
crystalclarity.com | clarity@crystalclarity.com
800.424.1055

ISBN   978-1-56589-117-3 (print)
ISBN   978-1-56589-535-5 (e-book)
Library of Congress Cataloging-in-Publication Data
   2022059307 (print) | 2022059308 (e-book)

Cover design by Tejindra Scott Tully
Interior design and layout by Michele Madhavi Molloy

The *Joy Is Within You* symbol is registered by Ananda
Church of Self-Realization of Nevada County, California.

"   "

• • • •

If you want to find the secrets of the universe, think in terms of **energy**, **frequency** and **vibration**.

Nikola Tesla

Concerning matter, we have been all wrong. What we have called matter is **energy**, whose **vibration** has been so lowered as to be perceptible to the senses. There is no matter.

Albert Einstein

People focus on genres of music and forget that **ENERGY** is the thing that transcends everything. And the **energy of community** and joy and of life...that life-affirming humanity that I love to present in my music is something that people really want.

Jon Batiste

What these numbers represent, beyond the obvious, is that **energy is moving**. And that's all we ever really need to know about anything in life: Is energy moving? The rest is then a matter of **directing that energy** towards a meaningful (and hopefully, uplifting) end.

Ana Maria (Narayani) Anaya
speaking about revenue at a new business.

[...T]he source of all life, as a constant, **unending flow of energy** that animates all of life. The terms "verb" and "process" best describe this reality. God's **energy flows everywhere**; it is how God "gods." We cannot control this energy; all we can do is recognize it and get in step with it, so that our very existence is in harmony with what is, rather than at cross-purposes with it. This orientation should help us align ourselves to all of creation, so that we can truly see the universe: the "uni"—the single **tide of energy** that ebbs and flows through creation—and the "verse"—the diverse array of manifest creations.

Rabbi Zalman Schachter-Shalomi *answering,*

In countless aspects of life, people will come to realize, as indeed they are doing already, that to tune in to the flow lessens one's need to be overly preoccupied with the details. It will become increasingly clear that, **inherent in the energy** itself, there exists a sort of guiding intelligence, rooted in an awareness higher than man's. Our awareness of that higher intelligence remains blocked as long as we allow our attention to be tumbled about by excessively numerous details. The flow will be released when our willpower is engaged in what we may describe as the natural rhythms of inspiration.

Swami Kriyananda, *Religion in the New Age*

Contents

Introduction

This is a book about working with energy. Yours and mine.

What do I mean by energy? Is it produced by the body metabolizing the calories we eat? Well, yes, partially. Is it the capacity to generate work? Yes, partially. Is it that which animates the body? Yes. Is it an inner life force of circulating energy like the Chinese concept of *chi*? Or the yogic concept of *prana*? Yes, that too. Is it something that each individual projects into the world, like magnetism or charisma? Is energy the same thing as vibration?

We know sound is made up of vibrations, so does that mean music is the same thing as energy? And when noted basketball star, Stephen Curry says, "The vibe in our locker room is real energetic and fun and real personable," is the "vibe" he mentions the same thing as energy? Then can mood be energy?

It is a little like talking about intelligence. When we speak of *intelligence*, do we mean that number that is measured by an IQ test? Do we mean one of the many types of intelligences outlined by Howard Gardner, such as linguistic or spatial? Is intelligence being able to learn a foreign language or the ability to repair a car? Or is *intelligence* the ability to learn from experience and change one's behavior?

Just as the word intelligence can represent multiple realities, so can the word energy. In fact, I would like to introduce one more unusual meaning for the word energy, and that is *willingness*. When we have more energy, we are more willing, and the opposite when we have less. I will discuss this further in chapters four and five.

To get the most out of the Keys to Energy in this book, it would be helpful to relax any rigid definition for energy and do your best to *feel* what is meant by the word in different contexts. In fact, it would be even better if you would begin to tune into people and events on a vibrational, or energetic level, behind words and actions. It is likely you already do this, perhaps unconsciously. You know which co-worker has negative critical energy and which one has energy that is light and playful. You may have thought of it as more personality than energy, but begin to notice how your own energy, or internal state, is affected by being with different individuals and in different environments.

This is a practical book with real-life experiences and real-life people (some names changed) that illustrate eight different keys to working on an energy level. Because my career has been in education, you will find many of my stories and examples concern children and teens, but the same principles apply with adults. You will find many practical suggestions that will ease tensions, improve your relationships, and create a happier environment—whether in your home, workplace, and/ or classroom.

Occasionally, we receive insights from unexpected sources if we really listen. A prospective parent was visiting our elementary school, considering enrolling her child. As she arrived, the students came outside for recess. She observed the children at play for a few minutes and then said, "The kids here are so calm compared to the children at my son's present school."

A few children *were* calmly playing in the sandbox, but most were actively playing and shouting, being normal children at recess. I understood that our classrooms were much calmer than most, but how could she see this on the playground?

"But most of them are running around; how can you tell?"

"Yes, but they are running with purpose, not just running wild. *They know where they are going.*"

One can recognize the difference between a moving, active child who is inwardly calm, and a moving, active child who is emotionally agitated. If you ask them to stop, the calm child can stop and be attentive in an instant. The agitated child is spinning on excitement and if you stop them, their minds and emotions are still racing; they are not centered enough in their bodies to pay attention to anything outside themselves.

In my first book, *Calm and Compassionate Children*, I explain how calmness and compassion are interrelated. When we are agitated or over-excited, we cannot clearly perceive the feelings or needs of others, nor can we learn anything new as readily as we can when we are calm and attentive. As J. Donald Walters says in *Education for Life,* "Our modern school system concentrates on imparting facts, but devotes far too little attention to developing a student's ability to absorb the information he receives."

I have heard the ideal state for learning described as "relaxed alertness." This ideal is as important for adults as for children. Most adults have learned, however, to set aside their worries and moods when they need to concentrate on a new challenge. Children need to have the experience of achieving this brain state. Experiencing it, they learn how it feels and how to recreate it. The more they experience it, the more those pathways in the brain are strengthened, and the easier it is to consciously opt for that state at will.

Focusing on behavior instead of consciousness or energy behind the behavior cannot solve the problem; it only amplifies it. Reason alone is not usually helpful for us to learn or achieve this calm, relaxed state as you will see in this book. It is a matter of energy and energy control. Yet, parents and teachers often act as though if they explain reasonably why a child should be calm or focused, it will resolve the matter. How often has that worked for you?

Where did these energy "keys" or precepts come from? I certainly did not figure them out on my own. In the mid-1980's I moved to an intentional yoga and meditation community in northern California, founded by Swami Kriyananda, a direct disciple of Paramhansa Yogananda. Yogananda was one of the early Indian emissaries who brought meditation to the West, arriving in Boston for the International Congress of Religious Liberals in 1920. He lived in the U.S. until his death in 1952. In addition to his mission of sharing the universal principles of yoga in the West, Yogananda had a special interest in education for children.

Two years after I began living at Ananda Village and teaching at the Kindergarten through eighth grade school established for residents' children, Swami Kriyananda, whose western name was J. Donald Walters, wrote and published the book *Education for Life*. (Where I quote from this book, I will use the name Walters since the book was published under his birth name.) He called *Education for Life* a "seminal" work, and urged us to use our own experience to elaborate on the ideas he offered. Education for Life is a philosophy and system that emphasizes the development of the whole child: body, feeling, and will, as well as intellect. Most importantly, it contains keys to working with others on an energy level, and how to motivate others relative to their energy level, or state of consciousness.

I worked at the Ananda Village Living Wisdom School for twelve years and then moved to Portland, Oregon. There I founded a Living Wisdom School in nearby Beaverton where I was the director for sixteen years. The experiences of the teachers, families, and students there were profound and life-affecting, helping me grow in understanding of the power of working with energy.

I am not necessarily the leading expert on this topic, but I am a super-enthusiastic advocate because I have experienced how tuning into these principles changed me, my classroom and the experience of my students in profound ways. Some first-readers of *Education for Life* may say, "Well, that is simple," and put the book down never to consult it again. Truth is simple, but not easy to live. I encourage you to read both *Education for Life* and this book looking for ways to apply these insights to your own life situations. I find that my understanding goes deeper each time I do this. It's a topic big enough for a life-long pursuit of understanding.

Awake and Ready is based on yogic ideas about energy and form, but most importantly, how to apply those ideas practically. I offer my understanding and experience to you in hopes that they may be helpful in your own relationships, whether with children, teens, family, co-workers, or even yourself!

Are you awake? Are you ready? Let's get started!

AWAKE AND READY

CHAPTER ONE

Excitement vs. Happiness (Energy Awareness)

Key 1: Engaged energy leads to contentment; merely excited energy often ends in disappointment.

Corollary: Seek to be calmly active and actively calm.

Excitement vs. True Happiness

As our school got out one afternoon, several shouting children were chasing each other around the playground, unable to contain their anticipation of an overnight birthday party. Watching them, one of the teachers commented, "Sometimes I think that parents confuse their children's excitement with happiness."

There is a profound truth behind that statement. Just as in nature every action has an opposite and equal reaction, so in human nature, every emotional mood swing upward has its opposite. Because the "happiness" (actually excitement) experienced by fulfilling a desire for something which lies outside of ourselves is transitory, there will inevitably be a corresponding emotional downswing.

How do *you* define happiness? Is it the sort of temporary high you experience when you get a new car or dress or fishing rod or electronic gadget? Is happiness the stimulation of ever louder music, ever-more suspenseful films, ever more friends, parties, sports events, and thrills? Corporate advertising which drives our media would certainly have us think so.

Or does your definition of happiness have more to do with contentment: the joy of quiet, inner calm that comes from self-acceptance, from being content in almost every circumstance, and from being able to recognize the needs of others and have compassion for them?

Observe a child who has been inundated with too many gifts at a special occasion or who is overstimulated at a theme park. They may speed-talk or run around restlessly without aim, unable to be still. Their relaxed laughter may become high-pitched and nervous. And, what happens soon afterwards? Within a day, or even a couple of hours, they will inevitably experience a crash from this emotional high. There will be dissatisfaction, whining, and even tears or a temper tantrum over some seemingly trivial disappointment. This type of excitement masquerades as happiness, but it leads to agitation, not contentment.

One might imagine the only alternative to a child who lives in this emotional maelstrom to be a bored child who is disinterested and dull. Nothing could be further from the truth. Children can be actively calm and calmly active—centered, happy, creative, and loving. This does not mean they are always quiet and still, but their activity has purpose and balance. As a result, people around them also enjoy their energy.

At a family camp one year, Michael (Nitai) Deranja, (founder of Living Wisdom Schools) and I decided to have the parents each share their favorite childhood memory as a way to get acquainted and engage their participation. It was really touching to hear others' precious childhood memories such as picking berries with their parents and making pies, canoeing on a lake on camping trips, spending the night with their grandparents, or making Christmas cookies every year.

I continued to do this at Education for Life workshops. Over the years, I have also asked colleagues and friends to share their memories with me. And I discovered that there were common themes in the vast majority of the answers: cooking, eating together, outdoor experiences, nature, solitude, family—especially parents and grandparents. Quite often, the experiences were activities that repeated year after year. No one ever gave an answer such as a fabulous birthday party or a big trip to Disneyland! And, amazingly, in all those answers over the years, *only one* person ever mentioned a gift or toy (a bicycle a parent hid in the yard for a Christmas surprise).

Notice and reflect on your own experience and those of people close to you. What has brought the greatest, lasting happiness? You may find that it is often experiences that involved awareness of being part of something bigger than oneself (the natural world) or connection with others—and contentment in the moment. It may not be the fast-paced thrills of driving ATVs or playing the latest computer game, but something deep and meaningful enough to always be remembered.

Friends of mine were looking for a hard-to-find rural property to buy, hoping to change their suburban lifestyle. They had been searching for several months when I ran into them at a local market. Thrilled that they had found just the place, the wife began telling me all about it. She was so excited that I could almost see sparks shooting out from her body as she chattered on and on about how perfect it was. I expressed happiness for them, but inwardly I got a very nervous feeling from her. Just a few weeks later, I heard the whole thing had fallen through after they spent more time on the land. They had found several problems, causing them to back out of the deal and lose their deposit. While I was very sorry for them, I wasn't surprised. Her energy seemed too ungrounded around this choice.

Learn to "Tune into the Energy"

If you quietly observe your children, in time you will begin to notice that certain games, music, and friends, that may initially produce what looks like happiness, really result in over-excitement leading to agitation. Other activities or companions nudge your child into that centered, relaxed state of consciousness that we all enjoy being around.

Take special note of when others are calmly happy, engaged and focused, open and receptive. In this state, whether doing an art project, dribbling a soccer ball, stacking blocks, or chatting with a friend, they are totally identified with the process, not the outcome. They are relaxed but entirely alert. Their eyes are soft, yet bright. The limbic system is calm and the higher brain centers are activated.

Mihaly Csikszentmihalyi, the well-known psychologist and one of the founders for the positive psychology movement, described this state, which he calls, "flow," as, ". . . being completely involved in an activity for its own sake. The ego falls away. Time flies. Every action, movement, and thought follows inevitably from the previous one, as in playing jazz. Your whole being is involved, and you're using your skills to the utmost." (Interview with *Wired* magazine.)

Being able to discern which activities result in inner contentment and which result in lack of focus can be your first step in helping your child to become calmly happy. Parents of younger children can exercise their discretion and, as much as possible, expose their child only to the most uplifting influences to help them develop the habits of inner calmness and self-control.

Of course, every child will experience some disappointments, some anger, some frustration and discouragement, but childhood does not have to be an out-of-control period of life. It is difficult for the brain to learn anything new when the body is experiencing a negative emotion. Everyone, child or adult, thrives and learns best in a state of relaxed alertness.

As children mature, you can help them become self-aware of when their energy is "off." You can help them to notice when they are becoming agitated and how to stop and breathe or step back from a situation. In a class of fourth and fifth-graders, I used to challenge the children to walk across the room balancing a book on their heads. It was fun, but also a practice that develops focus, concentration, and self-control.

One of the fifth-grade students simply could not understand the need to "settle down." One day, when he was beside himself, his inner agitation disturbing everyone, I told him that he needed to go outside and run to release his excess energy.

"No, I'm calm," he insisted.

"Okay," I replied, "if you're calm, show me you're in control by walking to my desk with a paperback book balanced on your head."

Grinning, sure he could do it because he had done it the day before, he put the book on his head and quickly started across the room. The book immediately fell off. He was stunned; he tried again, more slowly; it fell. Finally, he took a deep breath, and with concentration and will, he made it to my desk.

With this living demonstration, the entire class understood that it wasn't just an adult opinion that someone needed to get control of themselves. We had an objective measure! It was a great realization for him and the rest of the class.

If you can help your children recognize when their own energy fluctuates and what over-stimulates them, it will give them a lifelong tool for creating the life they want and for being able to follow through on their intentions. Even if they don't always make the ideal choices, the self-awareness you help them develop in childhood will not be forgotten and will be there for them to come back to as young adults.

Outward Behaviors Can Be Anticipated

I clearly remember the first time I was able to "tune into the energy" and recognize something was going wrong before it manifested itself outwardly. I walked by some kids I knew who were playing around on the lawn. They sounded particularly rowdy, so I paused to see whether they were fighting. But they were not, and so I went inside. In just a couple of minutes, I heard loud crying! Looking out the window, I saw that indeed someone had gotten hurt, either by accident or because a child had become too aggressive. I had actually intuitively known the energy was going in that direction because I had picked up on the voice tones and group dynamic.

I realized that if I could tune into the energy better in the classroom, I could perhaps intervene or shift what was happening *before* the energy manifested outwardly in lack of control, hurt feelings, an accident, or even just a distraction from our goal. Learning to tune in to the subtle (and sometimes not-so-subtle) cues of voice tone, nervous movements, and facial expressions gave me the opportunity to "change the energy" before it became impossible to stop. The rest of this book will give you many examples of how to do that, plus how to work with each child's energy to help them grow.

The Goal

In yoga, it is taught that the highest level of exis-tence is pure consciousness. Consciousness can man-ifest as energy, and it is energy that produces outward forms. Modern science has caught up to this truth: we know matter is not solid, but vibrating energy. When we learn to tune into the vibration or energy of others, whether as individuals or groups, we can help them more effectively, making our homes, class-rooms, committees, and workplaces more harmonious and effective.

Then, when we are able to tune into the energy flow of others, we can use the eight principles, or keys, in this book to:
- Create more harmony whether at home or in school;
- Help others focus on the tasks at hand;
- Get a reluctant student or employee started on something they find difficult;
- Minimize conflict and willpower struggles with kids;
- Increase children's and teens' ability to use their will to master challenges;
- Make school more fun;
- And, improve academic or other performance-based outcomes.

For teachers, it is crucial that they know how to help their students, no matter their age, become "Awake and Ready," actively calm, and calmly active. And for parents, understanding the difference between excitement versus happy, engaged energy will make all the difference in their children's ability to be attentive and content. For everyone, improving our ability to "read" our own energy and that of others is a step toward more awareness, more self-control, and more true happiness. It is a gift to those we love and to future generations.

Calmness is the only possible foundation for any true, lasting fulfillment and happiness. Calmness is possible only when the ego stops shouting for attention.

SWAMI KRIYANANDA, *Demystifying Patanjali*

CHAPTER 2

Nurture Enthusiasm

Key 2: Always nurture enthusiasm: the energy is more important than the details.

Corollary: You can help someone redirect their positive energy, but you cannot generate it for them once it's taken away.

Oh, No!

My eleven-year-old step-son, Phillip, was running toward the house excitedly calling my name. (We lived on four acres in the foothills of the Appalachian Mountains). He burst through the kitchen door and held up a gorgeous, but drooping, pink blossom. It was a lady slipper—the whole plant, roots and all!

"Look, what I found!" he cried. He knew I loved nature and especially wildflowers and his excitement was apparent.

But my reaction was not appreciative. "Oh, no, Phillip! You shouldn't have pulled the plant up out of the ground. It's a lady slipper—a rare wildflower."

Phillip's eager face fell. His enthusiastic and joyful energy completely deflated.

I felt so badly; he was just trying to share with me, and he didn't know better. I realized I had made a mistake, but I thought of it as only hurting his feelings. Later, I came to understand that taking someone's enthusiasm violates an important principle for living and for helping others develop their potential.

When people have energy, spirit, or enthusiasm for something, we should encourage that spirit, not deflate it—even when we are sure it is a bad idea! When someone first shares their enthusiasm is not the time to tell them the reasons their idea is impractical or to criticize the details. If you do that often to a child or an employee, it is likely that they will simply lose the will to create, to communicate with you, and/or to risk anything new.

I did quickly change course and hugged Phil and told him I loved it. But I needed to learn that one should never react to anyone's enthusiasm with a repressing energy. Ruining someone's enthusiasm is like stealing something precious. Even if you know that what they are proposing will not work, at least endorse their energetic investment in life. Later would be the time to share some sobering advice (if asked). And much later, when my step-son was not emotionally invested in my response, would have been the time to let him know that he should pick a flower, not pull it up by the roots.

Learn to Recognize the Enthusiasm of Others

After a family dinner with friends, I was impressed when the nine-year-old son got up from the table and began to clear the dishes. He smiled and chatted as he gathered the plates. But then, as he got to his mother's plate, she stopped him and began showing him how he was not picking the plates up in the most efficient way by removing the silverware to stack it on top.

As she corrected him, his face fell, and his shoulders sagged. He went from a smiling, competent person to an uncertain little boy who didn't want to pick up the stack again for fear he would do something else wrong. One moment he was in a flow of energy that was expansive and selfless, and the next moment his energy shrank to embarrassment. By focusing on his mistake rather than his positive energy, his mother discouraged him from helping in the future, although that was certainly not her intention. Next time, he would not likely volunteer for fear of embarrassment again by being told he was not doing it right.

Never squash someone's enthusiastic energy. *You can help someone redirect their positive energy, but you cannot regenerate it for them once you've taken it away.*

Always Encourage Positive Energy

As I began writing my first book, *Calm and Compassionate Children*, I was anxious for feedback. Among my questions: Is it readable? Are my arguments convincing? Did the writing flow? Is there a better way to organize the information? I shared my early writing with several readers.

One of them would say, "It's really good." While gratifying to hear, that response was not really helpful. Another friend would take what I wrote and proofread it. I'd get it back with all the grammar and punctuation corrected. I would have no idea if I were going in the right direction or whether my points rang true for her.

The feedback from a third friend was always encouraging. She never failed to find something positive to say about what I had written. Only then, she would tell me what part was confusing, or unclear. Her feedback always gave me a surge of energy and a direction to go next. Much later, when I read these same early versions, I could not believe how poorly written they were! I so appreciate this friend who saw the book's potential and nurtured my enthusiasm as I learned how to write. Without her encouragement, I might have abandoned the effort.

The fundamental importance of not blocking the flow of energy with criticism is practiced in brainstorming, a common business and education practice. If you have participated in brainstorming, you know that one of the cardinal rules is that you do not evaluate ideas as they come up. Often the energy flow generated by accepting the legitimacy of a stream of wildly impractical and seemingly unrelated ideas results in a creative solution arising into someone's mind.

When we respond positively to someone's enthusiasm—or at least neutrally, if being positive would be dishonest—we allow that person to explore their ideas and give them confidence that their thoughts deserve consideration. A negative reaction to someone's eagerness for an idea or project could even be considered stealing. Some people who would never think of taking a material object from another do not hesitate to throw cold water on someone's idea, in effect, stealing their energy. It is so easy to see what is wrong with an employee or a student and to think if we can just get them to correct those things, they will be successful. In the process of correction, however, we inadvertently trample on their energy and willingness. The focus on details must come later, after the person feels supported.

Look for Strengths

A parent of a preschool girl told me that the most important thing she gained from having her daughter at our school was to appreciate her daughter for who she was. She was focused on improving her child's weaknesses, such as difficulty sitting still and inability to concentrate on projects requiring attention to detail. We focused on the same child's vitality, zest for active play and sports, and the desire to be friends with her classmates. In the teacher's conversations with this mother, she affirmed these positive traits.

With the best of intentions, the mom had attempted to get her child to try harder at the things that were difficult. Feeling her mother's concern and sometimes exasperation, the daughter was starting to doubt herself, and becoming hesitant to even try learning her letters and numbers. In contrast, when she got into an environment that emphasized her beautiful qualities, she began to blossom again and to be willing to try the things that did not come easily. She became an exemplary student in the following years, and her mother thanked me for helping her see her daughter in a different light.

Thomas Edison was such a poor student in school that his teacher became completely frustrated with him. Rather than let his curious spirit be crushed, his mother took him out of school and homeschooled him. Would the outcome have been different if she had forced him to conform to the school or sent him to consultants and psychologists to try to help him fit into the mold of what the school expected? Would he still have had the passion for invention and belief that he could find the solutions he needed?

The Right Spirit

I have a friend who was an accountant, and a very good one. When she was hired to take over a small publishing company, I was surprised. She had no training and no experience in the field. But she was persistent, organized, brilliant, and really believed in the mission of the company. Within a few years, the company had attracted much success, and the former accountant became a master negotiator of foreign rights to the firm's books. Those who hired her understood the importance of the right energy; when it's there, the details will take care of themselves.

> Efficiency can be learned, but the right spirit can only be inborn, or at least inspired by good leadership.
>
> J. Donald Walters

When I became a principal, Karen, the first teacher I hired, had it all: the right education, the right experience, an expansive personality, and enthusiasm for an Education for Life school. The second teacher I hired was different. Helen had no teacher training and no experience in education, but she was all heart, and had an equal commitment to manifesting a more balanced model of education.

When I visited Helen's home, where she did some childcare for the neighborhood, I noticed she had dedicated the dining room wall—in her otherwise pristine, tastefully-decorated home—to a clothesline of art from her childcare displayed by clothespins. Helen was obviously organized, loved children, and her own children's eyes were full of light.

I asked Helen to be an aide in Karen's classroom. She quickly absorbed many successful techniques from observing Karen, the experienced teacher. Helen had a quieter personality than Karen and a beautiful rapport with her students; she inspired them to be their best selves.

Eventually, I invited Helen to teach kindergarten. She continued to further her own education, taking classes on teaching math and language arts. She could learn the skills she needed, but she had the right energy already, and Helen became a beloved teacher whom all the parents and students admired.

Finally, I think of Jane Goodall, the great paleontologist. When Louis Leakey hired her to observe chimpanzees in Africa, she had no apparent qualifications except her love of animals. After two years, he was so delighted with her work that he raised funds to send her to Cambridge to get the education needed for her research to command respect. The flow of energy generated by Leakey and Goodall set the course of her life. Everyone knows of her later accomplishments and her influence. She is the perfect example of this key, Nurture Enthusiasm!

In all cases, it is important to work with the child's strengths rather than concentrating on his weaknesses. Usually, he will respond far better to this positive approach.

J. Donald Walters, *Education for Life*

CHAPTER 3

Getting Unstuck: Action is the Answer!

Key 3: When the energy is "stuck," action is the answer.

Corollary: Almost any action is better than inaction — once the energy starts to flow, the momentum can be turned in the direction you wish to go.

Just Three Things

Sometimes after eating dinner, I feel lethargic. I look around the kitchen and think, "Oh, gee, look at this mess! I'm too tired to clean all this up."

So I tell myself, "I'll put away just three things,"

A body at rest tends to stay at rest.[*]

NEWTON'S LAW OF INERTIA, *a modern phrasing*

and I give myself permission to stop after three things if I want to. However, what happens, almost every time, is that after putting three things away, I'm "on a roll."

---

[*] Newton's actual words: The *vis insita*, or innate force of matter is a power of resisting, by which every body, as much as in it lies, endeavors to preserve in its present state, whether it be of rest, or of moving uniformly forward in a straight line. —Sir Isaac Newton, *Philosophiæ Naturalis Principia Mathematica*

I think, "Well, I'll just clean up the table or the counter before I stop." Pretty soon, I look around at how little is left and conclude, "Might as well finish now because it will feel great to get it done!" Five minutes earlier, I felt I just could not clean up the kitchen. What happened?

I got the energy moving!

It takes more energy to *begin* anything than to keep going once we've begun. Continuing to act is easy compared to getting started in the first place. It's Newton's law applied to people.

From Listless to Enthusiastic in a Moment

One of the most memorable instances I know of this principle at work involved Peter (Kabir) MacDow, a third/fourth grade teacher at Ananda Living Wisdom School. One morning he began class by singing a song with the kids. However, only one or two students were really singing, the others just dully sitting there.

So, he tried playing a little game to get their enthusiasm sparked. But they complained, "Do we have to?" (Every teacher has a dread of hearing that phrase!)

Finally, in complete exasperation at their unwillingness, Peter, with sudden inspiration, shouted, "Catch me if you can!" Then he ran out the door.

Bewildered, the children looked at each other. "What did he say?"

One ran to the window, "There he goes; he really meant it!"

"You're kidding," others said, jumping up to look. "He's really running off. Let's go."

By the time the children realized what had happened and got outside, Peter had a great head start, but he stopped and looked back, yelling, "You'll never catch me!" knowing this would incite them even more.

"Oh, yes, we will!" several shouted, everyone taking off after him.

Standing his ground, Peter taunted, "No, you can't," and turned and took off when the kids were only twenty yards away. He led them on a merry goose chase around the field, dodging them around the playground equipment until they finally divided up and caught him amid peals of laughter.

Breathlessly giggling and chatting, they all walked back to the classroom together. Everyone's mood had lifted, and Peter had their complete attention for his activities the rest of the day.

Overcoming inertia is difficult. In order to get the energy moving, it is okay, at first, to get it going in a *different* direction than desired. If necessary, you can then redirect it. For teachers, this principle is an essential key. For example, a tried-and-true technique to help recalcitrant students is to send them to take something to another classroom or the principal's office. When a student would show up in my office with a book I didn't want, I knew exactly what was happening. They would get an enthusiastic, "Thanks for bringing this over!" By the time they returned to the classroom they were almost always ready to join in the classroom flow. Getting them moving is so much more effective than explaining to children *why* they should cooperate.

Reason, emotional appeals, even threats—none of these work as well as just *moving* when one is stuck in inertia, unwilling and unable to act. When the energy is stuck, action is the answer.

Start Small

Just as I tell myself to just do three things when inertia is strong, children sometimes need a boost to get started. When a child refuses to begin a task, often it's because the task seems so overwhelming that they cannot raise their energy to meet it. In that case, often it works to give them a small success first. Break a task down into small parts, and ask them to do only the first step. For example, if it's a page of math problems, ask them to do just the first three. Give them praise for that and ask if they could do three more. Or if it is organizing their desks, have them just find all the trash and throw it away. You may discover that the energy generated by doing just a small piece of the task gathers momentum, and they can continue.

Writing teachers use this principle all of the time. When students are stuck, unable to think of what to write, the teacher tells them just to write (or type) *anything*—whatever they are thinking at the moment. Teachers may also get things moving by offering one sentence, or even just one word to get things going. Nine times out of ten, beginning to write "primes the pump," and students flow right into completing the assignment.

Just Ten Minutes

I had a chance to use this key of "action is the answer" at school one winter day when it began to snow. Kids get ultra-excited when it snows during the school day in areas where snow is uncommon. They run to look out the windows, chattering excitedly, hoping it will stick so they can sled and make snow balls. It is challenging to get them calmed down and focused on work again. Savvy teachers will often take them out to play, knowing that afterwards they will be able to concentrate better.

The snow began during silent reading time. Students begged to go outside, and I agreed. However, two students, both avid readers who were in the middle of good books, began to whine, "I don't want to go out." I was surprised that ten-year-old boys would object to playing in the snow, and I knew it would be good for them to play and get the fresh air and exercise. But to *make* them go play seemed a bit authoritarian. Besides that, you can't make anyone play!

Thinking of the axiom that once the energy is moving, it gets its own momentum, I told them, "Okay, you may read inside, but you have to go outside first and play for just ten minutes. After ten minutes, you can come back in if you want to." I suspected they would not want to go in; but if they did, they at least would have ten minutes of exercise.

Do you think they came back in ten minutes? No, a quarter of an hour later found them running, shouting, sticking out their tongues to catch snowflakes right along with the rest of the class. They were totally involved in the flow of the energy. When the kids returned to the classroom, every individual was happy and energized.

A Walk Gets a Seven-Year-Old Out of a Pout

Robbie came to my office for about the third time one October, both angry and sad that he was in trouble again.

I asked, "Why are you here?"

"The teacher sent me."

"What happened?"

He shrugged. Often when children have not been able to respect boundaries, resulting in an upset, they cannot speak. They are overcome with emotions such as guilt and anger that they cannot control. If you force them to talk, they will either cry or start to justify their side of the story, or invent complete falsehoods to try to escape the consequences of their actions.

Usually in an incident like this, I would offer the child a drink of water and have them sit down, telling them I will talk to them in a few minutes. I start playing calming music to slow down their heart and respiration rates and calm their minds and emotions. After five or ten minutes we talk about what happened and alternate ways to handle the situation next time.

But this child, I could see right away, was in a contractive state of self-pity and resentment and not moving through his emotions. I knew some of the reasons he might be having behavior problems (a diet too high in carbohydrates and processed foods and an erratic home schedule without regular sleep), and we were working on those with his parents, but what should happen right now? Inspiration struck: "Get him moving."

"Come on," I said, we're going to the library! He looked up, startled. I looked stern, "Come on, I have to go to the library, and I cannot just leave you sitting here, so you will have to go with me."

We walked outside down the sidewalk, and into the parking lot. As I shut the gate, I noticed that Robbie's expression had changed. Walking ten yards in the fresh air was already moving his energy. I said nothing. We had not gotten half-way across the parking lot before I heard a very quiet voice say, "I shoved Jason."

"What was that?" I said matter-of-factly, looking inquiringly at Robbie.

"I shoved Jason."

Now this was amazing. I had very seldom had a child volunteer information like this, and if they had, it would be accompanied by the inevitable, "But he called me a name!" or something similar.

"Ahh," I nodded sagely, slowing my pace. "What else happened?"

He talked about what happened as we walked through the park toward the library.

"How could you have handled it better?" I asked, and he gave a good answer (he had, after all, had practice at this!).

I returned my books, and we walked back, chatting amiably, where he apologized to his teacher and entered back into his classroom calmly. It amazed me to see him work through this process that we had been through before, but all on his own. He had a new sense of maturity about him from taking responsibility and apologizing without prompting.

Science tells us that physical activity actually helps us access the higher levels of our brains. I had discovered another tactic to add to my toolbox of helping kids who were shut down or caught in their own negative energy vortex: Get them moving so they could access the higher levels of their brains again.

This technique works just as well with a group as with an individual. When children begin to tire or look bored, help them regain their focus with action. For instance, toss a beanbag to students when you ask a question, and have them toss it back when they answer. Or play a quick game, for example, Simon Says (just for fun; no one ever is "out"), a clapping game, or Scrambled Anatomy.

If you are working with a group of adults, you can have them stand up and stretch, do a standing yoga posture, or clap to some music. Even asking a few quick questions where people have to raise their hand will produce an instant "reset" of the energy—and therefore the attentiveness and receptivity of the group. Don't take my word for it; try it. Action is the answer!

The bridge from mental dullness to higher awareness is constructed of intense activity of some kind. Of no use to the self-involved child are such expansive techniques as visualization, meditation, and positive thinking. None of these "light" activities can address the reality of a wholly negative attitude.

J. DONALD WALTERS, *Education for Life*

CHAPTER 4

Energy Follows Will

Key 4: Energy flows where there is willingness.

Corollary: The greater the will, the greater the flow of energy — to lead others, tune into their interests and motivations.

Paramhansa Yogananda said, "The greater the will, the greater the flow of energy!" The amount of energy, perseverance, concentration, and enthusiasm we can summon up for anything depends on our willingness to embrace it as ours to do. Imagine that you have had a really tough week at work. Your apartment is cluttered, the dishes unwashed, but you are exhausted. You put on your robe, order in a pizza, and lie on the couch to watch a video. Suddenly, the phone rings and you see it is your mother.

"Hi, Hon. Your dad and I unexpectedly had to come out to drop off a package to one of his clients, and we thought we'd stop by and give you some homemade peach pie."

"Thanks, Mom!" and in a flash, you are off the couch, clearing up the pizza, washing the dishes, and hiding the trash. What happened? How could you go from too tired to do anything to a whirlwind of activity in a moment? The energy was available; it was the will to direct it that you lacked.

I had a colleague who loved sports and aerobic exercise. She was always trying to get me to participate with her, but my idea of sport was skiing—no effort; just stay balanced and enjoy the ride! One spring our school had a mini track meet, and we were figuring out some averages and times together. Ten students had run a race and we wondered what their average time was. Impatiently she said, "Oh, that's too complicated to do right now."

"No, we just have to add the times up and divide by ten," I replied.

"That's two steps!"

"Yeah, but we don't really have to divide; since there are ten kids, we just more the decimal over one."

"Too complicated." She was already moving off, exasperated. I was puzzled, wondering why she wouldn't wait for me to put thirty seconds' effort into finding out what we both wanted to know. Then I laughed because I realized that this must be how puzzled she was about me when I refused to play tennis or go for a run, fun and easy activities for *her*. Just as I had little willingness for that sort of physical activity, she had little will for a mental math task, even if it were as simple (to me) as adding up a few numbers and moving a decimal.

When it comes to students, we understand that they have differing talents and academic abilities. We attempt to be patient with their differences. Good teachers go further, and design ways to motivate students in a variety of ways. For example, an elementary teacher may have her students write "number stories" (which we used to call *word problems*) such as, "If three bunnies were playing and six more joined them, how many bunnies were there?" and then draw and color pictures to illustrate the "story." Most children like the drawing part, and it makes the intellectual challenge more within their reach. Because this age child is in the "Feeling Years" (ages six to eleven, a stage described in *Education for Life*), using animals for math and letting children draw them is ideal.

Some kids like to be very active and need to move often. Good teachers keep all students more engaged by employing movement in their lessons to motivate them to stay on track. For instance, at the middle-school level, one can have them stand up (not just raise their hands) if a statement about a topic is true or squat by their desks if false. The kindergarten teacher I described in Nurture Enthusiasm had her children write down words they were learning by posting each word on an index card in different spots around the room. Students had to walk to each word, try to memorize the spelling, and return to their desks to write the words down. They could go back as many times as needed. What an innovative activity to combine physical and mental skills! And how motivating to those students who would never want to practice spelling in their seats.

In the elementary school years, while students are motivated by feeling, they love stories that stimulate their hearts, such as *Charlotte's Web*, *Babe*, and *Wonder*,

all of which were made into films. This natural incli-
nation toward stories can be used to help students engage in subjects that do not appear to have feeling built
in, such as math or topics in science. A story about a
particular dandelion seed and its life cycle draws them
right in (*The Dandelion Seed* by Joseph Anthony) where
a mere description of its life cycle can be dry and dull.

It is possible to use the interests and enthusiasms
of students to motivate them in almost every subject by listening sensitively to what topics engage
the students and incorporating those topics in some
way. Certain age levels tend to universally enjoy some
topics, such as mammals, reptiles, dinosaurs, and silly
puns. I know a first-grade teacher who created a moon
unit for her class. All kids can relate to the moon and
are curious about what makes its shape change. For this
age, however, her approach is not merely factual. They
read a story where a bear and the moon are friends who
talk to one another; they have a full-moon celebration
where they recite the poems they've learned and eat
"moon cookies." They are motivated to learn about
gravity, centrifugal force, and more because they are
drawn into the activities through their *hearts*, as well
as their minds.

I had a combined fifth and sixth-grade class for
English, and we had finished a unit where they each
read a biography on a prominent person in a field they
were interested in; for example, I chose Beatrix Potter
for a girl who loved art and illustrating stories. They
participated, but they were not as enthusiastic as I
had hoped. Talking about what to read next, they told

me, "The primary class is studying mythical creatures like the sphinx and dragons!" They said this with such *longing*.

Startled by their plaintive tone, I realized that they yearned to immerse themselves in something magical. So I chose Monica Furlong's *Wise Child*, which has elements of fantasy, and also appreciation of nature, compassion for others, and a friendship between a boy and a girl that is not romantic. All of these appealed to and uplifted this class. They loved it and did all sorts of related projects such as reports on herbs, drawing herb gardens, and writing a sequel. Be flexible! When you pay attention, you will perceive clues to give others the benefit of their own natural willingness.

Will Increases with Choice

Very young children come to school enthusiastic about almost everything. If they have teachers who know how to enter their world, build on their interests, help them make connections, and keep them active, they will continue to be willing and eager right up through the middle elementary years. As they approach puberty, they become more interested in exerting their own will.

Very young children thrive on routine and predictability, but as they grow and mature, we want them to use their own reason and intuition. Giving them

> Willpower is that which changes thought into energy.
>
> SWAMI KRIYANANDA,
> *The Essence of the Bhgavad Gita*

opportunities to choose helps them practice those
skills. Sometimes we forget how regulated students'
lives are and how much of school consists of doing
what they are told to do. Even choosing between just
two alternatives requires them to activate their own
willpower. Anytime we can use our creativity to give
them some power over their assignments increases the
likelihood of their putting their energy into action.
Examples of choices that could be offered:

- You can have oatmeal or toast and almond butter
  for breakfast.
- You can write a report on Rachel Carson or on
  Jane Goodall.
- For your weekly chore you can mow the lawn, do
  the family laundry, or wash the car.

Notice that choices are not open-ended, and that
the younger the child, the fewer the choices. Questions
like, "What do you want for breakfast?" and "Write
a report on a scientist," are much too general and can
lead to decision paralysis.

Multiple studies have shown that students are
more engaged when they have choices. You can Google
"benefits of student choice" and find numerous arti-
cles and studies cited. When our will is engaged by
making a choice, our energy level increases. As the corollary of this key tells us, "The greater the will, the
greater the flow of energy." Being told to take out the
trash is having someone else's will imposed on us; getting to choose whether to take the trash out or empty
the dishwasher engages our own will.

More and more schools in the U.S. have their seniors do a semester-long "senior project" investigating a topic, and perhaps building or creating something that is of interest to them. Choices can also be incorporated on a daily basis. For example, an English teacher may want to teach the sonnet. Instead of assigning one Shakespeare sonnet, they might give students the choice between two or three to read and be able to paraphrase. A fifth-grade teacher might give students studying birds the choice of making clay models of the three types of bird feet, or of taking photographs of birds at a bird feeder and using several for an informational poster. Even such a small choice as, "You may *sit* at the front of the room to give an oral report or you may *stand* at your desk," will help some students be more willing to put their energy into their delivery. In my later years of teaching, I learned that giving students three discussion questions on an exam with the instructions to choose two to answer produced more interesting and thoughtful answers by far.

Remembering to provide children and young people (oldsters too!) with plenty of opportunities for healthy exercise through sports, noncompetitive games, hikes, skiing, bicycling and so on also plays a role in having the energy to apply to other areas of their lives. Affirmations, too, can play a part. The Superconscious Living Exercises, available on the **ananda.org** website, include positive statements, such as, "I am awake and ready!" and "I am master of my body; I am master of myself!" Saying these affirmations along with the

accompanying movements imprints in the mind attitudes that bring life success.

Of course, if we expect children and teens to be able
to introspect and apply their willpower to their actions,
we must be willing to do so ourselves. What we *are*
speaks much more loudly to others than what we *say*.
So, I will end with these guidelines for developing will.
These are important practices both for our own growth
and for guiding us in our interactions with others.

1. LOOK ALWAYS FOR SOLUTIONS,
instead of concentrating too much
on your problems.

2. LOOK FOR GOODNESS IN
PEOPLE; don't concentrate on their
faults.

3. SET YOURSELF SPECIFIC TASKS TO
ACCOMPLISH — small ones at first,
then increasingly challenging ones.
Be sure to see each one through to
completion.

SWAMI KRIYANANDA, *Rays of the Same Light, #40*

Another aspect to consider in tapping into others'
willingness to put out energy is the individual's Specific
Gravity, the topic of the next chapter. Some students

love to connect with others (enjoy group activities), some like music when they do art, some love a pat on the back; others prefer a wink or smile. Others may need no feedback at all; they enjoy an activity for its own sake. Understanding people's abilities to harness their energies for challenges and using that understanding to motivate them is a characteristic of all great leaders, whether they are conscious of it or not.

Willpower is the driving force behind the flow of energy. And if it's true that "the greater the will, the greater the flow of energy," we need to give people those things that will reinforce their will, and not paralyze it, and not discourage or dishearten them. Encourage them in their strengths, as I said. Be truthful in encouraging their higher truth, and you will be doing them the favor of being a true friend.

SWAMI KRIYANANDA, *The Art of Spiritual Counseling*

CHAPTER 5

I Can't. Why Should I? I Will! (Progressive Development)

Key 5: Motivation varies according to the level of energy.

Corollary: You enhance the flow of energy when you use the motivation appropriate for the level of Specific Gravity.

What is Progressive Development?

> All mankind is divided into three classes: those who are immovable, those who are movable, and those who move!
>
> BENJAMIN FRANKLIN

Why is it that one person desires to be helpful, while another is helpful only when the outcome is personally beneficial? Why does one student take advantage of free afterschool tutoring to raise their SAT score while another says, "I am not wasting my free time doing more math!" Why does one person use their money to fund restoration of the rainforest while another lives a lavish and hedonistic lifestyle with their wealth?

After all, everyone is looking for the same thing in life—happiness.

But we do not agree on how to get happiness. For example, say there are three people who see someone drop several hundred-dollar bills. All three of them have modest means and could really use a financial windfall. Sanjay picks up the bills, and runs after the owner to give it back. He cannot imagine keeping it for himself. Rosa grabs the money and calls out to the owner in order to return it, hoping for a reward. Tony really wants to pick it up and keep it but sees a shopkeeper watching and walks on because he does not want to get in trouble with the police. Each one has a different motivation according to their level of personal development: Sanjay is motivated by truth; Rosa is motivated by rewards; and Tony is unmotivated, except to avoid pain.

> Each person is on a continuum of awareness, learning how to find happiness, and . . . happiness increases in direct proportion to the expansion of empathy and in inverse proportion to the contractive density of self-affirmation.
>
> J. DONALD WALTERS,
> *Education for Life*

If we want to motivate others to grow in maturity—socially, emotionally, and spiritually—it is essential to understand how motivation changes depending on one's level of awareness and energy. We would need to approach Sanjay, Rosa, and Tony very differently. Which of the three is closer to discovering the key to happiness? From your own personal experience, think of the most self-centered, selfish person you know and compare them to someone you know who is kindhearted, generous, and interested in others. Who is happier?

We call this continuum of awareness Progressive Development: Everyone is on this continuum and will react to the same situation according to their Specific Gravity, a term for their level on the continuum. We can see the maturity continuum reflected in our development from childhood to mature adulthood. The baby knows nothing but its own needs, but the toddler may offer a bite of food to the parent. The toddler may comfort another child who is crying; the teen may have the desire to help refugees or the homeless. However, some may never get to that level and think mostly of themselves.

What Are the Three Levels of Specific Gravity?

Although Specific Gravity falls on a continuum of subtle gradations of awareness, we can roughly divide the continuum into three categories: Light, Ego-active, and Heavy. For those who have studied the philosophy of yoga, the three stages correspond to the three *gunas*: *sattva*, *rajas*, and *tamas*.

This is a *continuum* of awareness that moves from contraction toward expansion, from heaviness toward lightness, and from self-centeredness toward the "sympathetic acceptance of the realities of others" (*Education for Life*) as shown in the following chart.

PROGRESSIVE DEVELOPMENT CONTINUUM

Specific Gravity	Attitude	Motivation
Light	I will!	To seek truth and help others
Ego-Active	Why should I?	To be rewarded
Heavy	I can't.	To avoid pain

The Three Levels of Specific Gravity

The flower bulb on the bottom at the Heavy level of Specific Gravity represents potential, but that potential is dormant and undeveloped. Although the bulb may look lifeless, the capacity for its unfoldment into a beautiful flower is there, just as every person has the possibility of soul fulfillment.

As the energy increases (in humans, actually moving up the spine), the self begins to develop. Leaves convert sunlight into energy that is then used for its own further growth. The plant is thriving, but all of its energy is going into its own self-development.

Finally, at the Light level, the flower blossoms. The plant realizes its divine potential: the flower releases its beauty and fragrance for all to enjoy. It gives its gifts to all who come—there is no holding back—it exists for joy itself. Let's look at how each level looks in the people we know.

We call the energy of those whose sympa-
thies are expanded most outside themselves, not only to their own family and
community, but to all mankind, indeed,
to all creatures, "*Light.*" This type of
person will happily be of assistance to a classroom or group—cleaning up after a meeting,
bringing refreshments, organizing an agenda. In addition to being motivated to help others, someone with
Light energy has a desire to seek truth and beauty. They
like to learn for the joy of learning. They may even be
light in their movements, and certainly there is mental
flexibility and the ability to take in new information
and to change and evolve. In the Light state of energy
or consciousness we include others in our happiness,
and we enjoy an activity for itself rather than for a reward or outcome only.

The next category of Specific Gravity we call,
"*Ego-Active.*" In the Ego-active state we want, even if
only subconsciously, a reward for our effort.
That reward may be tangible or monetary, or
it might consist of praise or recognition. For
teens and children, time on electronic devices
is a motivating reward. In this state, people
have energy and enthusiasm, but mainly use
it for their own gratification. When we are in
an Ego-active state, we may help with cleanup,
but mainly so that others will recognize our con-
tributions or because we want to feel a sense of
belonging to the group.

And finally, there are those who seldom or never contribute, either materially or energetically. They are negative and contractive. We call this level of energy, *"Heavy."* In this state, people are simply unmotivated by anything except to avoid pain. They may be able to hold down a job because they do not want to be homeless, but the effort they put into doing the job well would be minimal. Step by step, they have to learn that they can improve their situation with energy. The bulb begins to suck up water and convert its dormant energy into upward growth, seeking Light.

These three energetic levels have been identified by many others, for example, researchers in the field of moral development such as Lawrence Kohlberg, and educators such as Rafe Esquith, a recipient of the National Teacher-of-the-Year Award and the National Medal of the Arts. Esquith said that in every class he could identify three groups. There are a few who do not want to learn and are practically impossible to motivate and a few who are eager, enthusiastic, and energetic. Finally, the largest group is one that can go either way—willing participation or boredom. He concentrates his attention foremost on challenging the most energetic and willing students (Light) because he knows when he gets them engaged, the other two groups will come along too. These observations are coherent with the Education for Life philosophy: those experiencing Light Specific Gravity will help those at the Ego-active level be more expansive. Also, those in an Ego-active energy state can often get those with less energy to participate.

Some divide the Ego-active stage into two stages: Ego-Active/Contractive and Ego-Active/Expansive. In the Ego-active category, when close to Heavy, the person is motivated by tangible reward for themselves. Rising into the higher Ego-active level, we can be motivated by rewards for our family, and even our community. But the motivation sought is still external; motivation is not entirely internally driven until in the Light Specific Gravity stage.

Actually, every level could be further subdivided, because it is a continuum. Think of ice melting; it turns to water gradually. At some point it is a mixture of both ice and water. Then water becomes warmer and warmer, until it evaporates into vapor. Or think of how the color spectrum transposes from one color to another.

Identifying the Three Levels of Energy

LIGHT SPECIFIC GRAVITY: I WILL!

When we willingly participate and cheerfully do our part, we are acting from *Light Energy*. We are internally motivated. In this state of consciousness, we are aware of the needs of others and take them into consideration in our actions. We often go the extra mile because we enjoy our work for its own sake. Our physical energy is under our control, and we focus deliberately. To help you visualize each level, I will use examples from *Winnie the Pooh* and also from the educational TV series, *Sesame Street*. You can find videos of them on YouTube.

In the *Winnie the Pooh* books, Milne creates Christopher Robin—a Light character who solves every problem and reassures and uplifts all the others. Another perfect depiction of this stage of energy is optimistic and willing Elmo of *Sesame Street*. Both Christopher and Elmo are interested in everyone and expansive in their energy. When we are feeling Light, we are aware of realities other than our own. Children with this awareness often gaze upward, enjoy a challenge, and are attracted to friends of a similar consciousness.

EGO-ACTIVE SPECIFIC GRAVITY: WHY SHOULD I?

Many times we act because we want the approval of others or because we want to get paid or obtain some other tangible gain. Externally motivated, we look to see what we will get out of our efforts. While we *may* consider the happiness of others, such as our family or neighbors, we are little concerned with people outside the group we identify as ours. We have energy, but it will often be unfocused and restless. Cookie Monster in *Sesame Street* and Tigger in *Winnie the Pooh* personify (so to speak) this level of energy that we call *Ego-Active*. At the bottom of the Ego-active level there is energy, but it is often unfocused, as is Tigger, bouncing around with no awareness of how he is affecting others. When we are higher on the continuum of the Ego-active energy, we sometimes may unselfishly help others, and we may be generally benevolent like Pooh. At its very lowest, this Specific Gravity includes the egoist who does *nothing* for unselfish motives. Therefore, they may be inharmonious with those around them, as their desires will inevitably clash.

Have you ever had a task you dreaded? Finishing your taxes or mowing the lawn on a hot day, for example? And did you ever offer yourself an incentive, such as, "I'll go out to a movie tonight, but only after I've worked three hours on this"? Just telling ourselves we *ought* to do it is simply not enough. Sometimes we need to use techniques to motivate the Ego-active level and so we offer ourselves a reward to get motivated. For example, "I will get a snack when I finish this task." Other times the motivation may be less tangible: the approval of a parent or the happiness on a child's face when we play with them.

HEAVY LEVEL SPECIFIC GRAVITY: I CAN'T.

If you are reading this book, you probably do not experience the *lowest* level of energy very often. At the *Heavy* level of Specific Gravity, there is little motivation to do much of anything. In this low energy state, we are completely unaware of the realities of others. We may be negative, depressed, or simply unmotivated. In Heavy Specific Gravity, even tangible rewards do not seem worth going after; only the threat of pain can get us moving. Heavy energy (that is, latent energy, needing to be awakened) may be a personal characteristic, but this state can also be a temporary condition. Even very Light individuals can experience a Heavy level of Specific Gravity—for example, due to ill health, a poor diet, or life trauma. A usually willing and eager child whose family is going through a difficult divorce may become listless and unmotivated, even though that is not their natural Specific Gravity.

To imagine this state, think of Eeyore from *Winnie the Pooh* or Oscar the Grouch from *Sesame Street*. The cartoonists Jerry Scott and Jim Borgman also depict this stage with their amusing comic-strip character, Zits. Imagine a young teen going through puberty, slouched on the couch, drinking soda, watching movie after movie until the wee hours and then sleeping-in the following morning, and you will have a really good idea of what this energy (or lack of it) looks like. His Specific Gravity is so low that he sits low on his spine, exasperating his parents with his indolence.

The best way to identify someone's Specific Gravity is by using one's own calm, intuitive feeling. However, there are objective signs to watch for: body language, choice of friends, and response to challenges.

HOW EACH STAGE REACTS TO A CHALLENGE

LIGHT
I will!   "I'll give it my best!"   "Sure!"
                                                "Let's figure it out."

Ego-Active
Why should I?   "Do I have to?"   "What's in it for me?"
                                                "You show me how."

HEAVY
I can't.   "I hate to do that!"   "Okay, (but I don't plan
                                                      to follow through.)"

It would be great if we could perform *all* of our duties out of the pure desire to seek truth or to help others, but depending on the circumstance, we may experience all three levels of energy even in the same day! A child may exhibit a Heavy state when told to do their homework, a Light state when offered the opportunity to play soccer, and an Ego-active state when asked to share their art supplies.

If we are honest, we can probably see all of these three stages at different times within ourselves. After I signed a contract on my first book, I was so motivated that I had no trouble sticking to a writing schedule. But, by the time I was working on the final chapters, I was so tired of the process, that I would sit at the computer and just stare at the screen for a while. Then I would decide I needed a snack or I had a call to make, or even an urge to clean house! Analyzing myself, I knew I was hovering between Heavy and Ego-active in this task. Well, I made a rule for myself: I could only get up from the computer and have a break when I had written four pages or edited eight. After I had done that, I could make a cup of tea and relax for ten minutes. That self-imposed reward helped me get back on track when the desire to help others (Light) or the desire to keep my advance (Ego-active) were not enough!

One can see examples of the three main stages of Specific Gravity everywhere, for example, in music, in the comics, and in other media. While advertising usually uses either Heavy (avoidance of pain—people will laugh at you if you have a slow cell phone) or Ego-active motivation (people will admire you if you drive this cool car), I have noticed more and more advertising using Light motivation. For example, my local public radio station used to offer only "gifts" such as mugs and tote bags in exchange for donations. A year ago, they added another option—a donation to the local food bank. This is a classic example of going beyond the Ego-active to offer rewards at the Light energy level.

Working with Specific Gravity Levels

The ability to identify these three levels of energy or awareness and work with each differently is a skill all teachers, managers, and executives need. In fact, very successful people use many of these principles, although they may not articulate them. Looking at the chart above, "How Each Stage Reacts to a Challenge," you may see that an effective leader will be able to flow through different management styles, according to the person or group they are trying to motivate.

When employees or students are acting from a Heavy level, one has to be more authoritarian and make a rule such as, "You will receive your paycheck after your time sheet is filled out and signed." (It is best to phrase it in this manner rather than, "You won't get your pay until you turn in your time sheet," because just phrasing the same outcome as a reward, not a punishment, can help nudge this person into seeing that they must put out energy to receive the rewards they want.)

When working with people acting in Ego-active energy, your discrimination and creativity can come more into play. What motivates this particular person? I knew a kindergarten teacher who loved to take her kids on nature walks, but one little girl would lag behind and eventually sit down and refuse to go farther unless carried. The teacher tried many tactics, but the one that finally worked was, "If you walk the whole way two days in a row, I will take you home with me after school to meet my kitty." The child got excited about that and had no trouble keeping up. And subsequently it was not a problem at all. So, the manager or teacher becomes a close observer: what does this person want or enjoy and how can I use that to help them overcome their unwillingness?

And, when working with those with Light Specific Gravity, you will find that you only have to provide direction and opportunities for expansion and growth, and those you are responsible for will discover more and more ways to learn and/or serve. You are a director rather than a "boss," and a catalyst who provides ideas and inspiration. They will begin to contribute their own ideas and hints of directions that you can explore together.

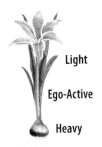

LEADERSHIP STYLE

Light	Co-creator, Catalyst
Ego-Active	Inspirer, Fair distributor of praise, grades, celebrations
Heavy	Authority figure

Finally, when working with a group, it is important to spend most of your energy motivating those with Light and Ego-active energy because they themselves with their own magnetism will bring the less inspired ones along. It is a mistake I have seen too often among teachers that they concentrate their focus on the most reluctant students instead of inspiring those with Light energy or leadership ability. The class becomes bored, and so much potential for growth is lost.

Being Realistic

In helping others, whether it be our children, our family members, or our employees, it is important to remember this universal principle: We can only take our *next* step. Maybe during a period of inspiration we can rise to a higher level—where we experience our oneness with all and are permeated with joy—but eventually, we come back to our own Specific Gravity and have to do the work of self-improvement to climb to the level we glimpsed.

Employers, parents, and teachers frustrate themselves and others by having unrealistic expectations and demanding that others perform at a level too far beyond where they are. An example of this is asking an out-of-control child to sit down and listen. Focused listening is not the next step after out-of-control behavior! Rather, we want first to get the child's attention to help them take control of their energy. *Then* we can ask them to listen.

Another example of asking someone to reach too high is when an adult forces a child to apologize when they are in a contractive state. It is asking them to skip over Ego-active right up to Light Specific Gravity; they cannot do it sincerely and end up resenting the act of apologizing. Better to verbalize what the child might be feeling, "You may have been afraid that if you didn't push her aside, you wouldn't get a turn." Add a reassurance, "We can always figure out a way to be fair to everyone." And leave it at that. If an apology is needed, wait until the child is in an Ego-active state and able to be somewhat sincere at least.

In our daily lives as spouses, parents, and employers, we are too often lazy and default to a threat rather than creatively thinking of how to motivate positively. Sometimes it is just a matter of changing our language: Instead of, "If you don't eat your dinner, you will NOT get dessert!" try a calmer statement, "If you eat your dinner, you can have ice cream with us afterward." (Of course, you have to follow through consistently for these statements to be effective . . . but that's the topic of another book.)

It is also counterproductive to use a type of motivation lower than the Specific Gravity you are dealing with. My friend was a well-paid and smart employee who worked for a high-tech startup company located in an office building that had restaurants and a gym on the ground floor. He was furious when he got a memo requiring him to park in the parking garage rather than in the lot which had roomier spaces and was easier to exit. He complained bitterly.

A few months later, we drove by the building, and I asked whether he had adjusted to the parking. "Oh, sure," he exclaimed. "

"What changed?"

"The owners of the gym and restaurants came to our staff meeting and explained to us how much they needed those visible spaces for customers. I really want them to stay in business, so I don't mind the inconvenience!"

This is a good example of the downfall in treating people who have Light or nearly Light consciousness in a Heavy manner. Being ordered not to do something just "got his back up" and made him want to rebel. On the other hand, being asked to help others motivated him and completely reversed his attitude because his Specific Gravity was Ego-active moving toward Light.

Incentives are Better than Threats

Nick, a parent and owner of a successful "geek help" business, worked on the school office computers in partial trade for tuition. One day he told me that his employees were really angry, and a couple had threatened to quit.

"What happened?" I asked.

"Well, the guys have to keep records of their calls so we can be sure we are actually making a profit and keeping everyone busy. They kept forgetting to write calls down, and turned reports in late.

"That was no way to run a business, so I made a rule that anyone turning in their paperwork late will be docked two hours pay for the next payroll period."

To Nick this seemed to be a fully justified tactic, but to me it looked like he was using a Heavy level of motivation to motivate Ego-active employees. Nick had taken our Education for Life class on motivating children so I was comfortable using this language to discuss it.

"I can see why the employees are upset, Nick. When you try to motivate people and you start with the lowest form of motivation—avoiding pain—people who are not Heavy are bound to resent it. You wouldn't have hired any of your people if they were Heavy."

"Yeah, but I did explain over and over why it was important that they fill out the forms, and it never did any good!"

"Well, that's the approach for people whose energy is Light—appealing to their desire to help you. But if that does not work, the next level is the Ego-active

state in between Heavy and Light—those who are motivated by rewards or self-interest. Is there any way
you could have offered something that would motivate
employees to fill out the forms, rather than threaten to
punish them if they didn't?"

"Oh, gee," Nick groaned. "I should have offered the
employees who get their paperwork in on time a paid
hour *off*. I could afford it, if I could just get things more
organized by having those reports!"

To Reward or Not?

Some child development experts say that it is better not to reward children as rewards encourage external
rather than internal motivation. This premise sounds
logical and true, but is it *universally* true? Rewards *can*
be misused if they are used with students who are already willing and able. This takes the spirit right out of
the action that the person is already willing to do.

We know that the same rules do not apply at every
stage of growth. When a child is twelve months old and
wants something unhealthy, we divert his attention;
when he is twelve years old, we may explain why it is
not good for him. When a two-year-old cries because
she does not get something in a restaurant, we may
pick her up and hug her. When she is nine and does the
same thing, we would have a different reaction.

Similarly, the way we approach people at different
levels of Specific Gravity should allow for the different
needs at each stage. When someone has trouble raising
their energy to accomplish something, a reward can be
a kick-starter to get over their own resistance so their

energy can flow. Once that resistance is resolved, the person often continues in that higher flow.

One of our teachers at Living Wisdom School used to draw a cursive letter on each student's back as they practiced writing the letter. Eight-year-old Harry struggled when it was time for handwriting. He would wiggle in his seat, play with his pencil, and make faces at other children. His teacher tried reminders to focus. No change.

He said, "It's too hard." She encouraged him and told him she knew he could do it. No change. She cut back his recess . . . no change.

One day the teacher noticed how much Harry loved having her trace the letters on his back and how still he sat. When he asked her to do it again, she said, "I'll come back and write it on your back five times after you write a whole line of letters on your paper."

He immediately bent to the task. The restless unhappy child suddenly became focused. Each time he finished a line, the teacher traced the letter on his back again. As the days went by, he would often forget to ask for reinforcement when he came to the end of each line. Just getting him started with a reward helped him to overcome his resistance, and the reward was eventually not needed.

We see these principles demonstrated in an activity called Rocks in the Basket. A rock is put in a small basket each time someone in the classroom is helpful in any way. Students or the teacher can do this, but no rock can be put in the basket if the child doing the helpful act draws attention to it himself. When the basket is full, the class has a little celebration or special treat such as a nature walk, double read-aloud time, or free play. Children learn through experience that it is enjoyable to be in a classroom where students are helpful, and before long, they don't even ask for rocks in the basket, but just effortlessly continue the culture of kind consideration for others.

This is what we find more times than not. When we use rewards at the right time, when we see a child is not aware of their own ability, a reward to "kick start" their energy will often get them moving. Once an activity is started, the feeling of accomplishment is enjoyable and the reward becomes irrelevant.

In Walter Isaacson's biography of Steve Jobs, Jobs recalls getting a reward from his fourth-grade teacher, whom he called Teddy and describes as "one of the saints of my life."

Apparently he was not a very good student. "After school one day, she gave me this workbook with math problems in it, and she said, 'I want you to take this home and do this.' And I thought, 'Are you nuts?' And then she pulled out one of these giant lollipops that seemed as big as the world.

"She said, 'When you're done with it, if you get it mostly right, I will give you this and five dollars.' And I handed it back within two days." After a few months he no longer required the bribes. "I just wanted to learn and to please her."

He continues: "I learned more from her than any other teacher, and if it hadn't been for her, I'm sure I could have gone to jail."

Jobs gives Teddy credit for *transforming his life.* Perhaps he was bored by school, but whatever the cause of his lack of enthusiasm, the surprising offer of a lollipop and money kick-started his motivation. Once his energy was flowing through the doorway of his talent, he could feel her regard for him, and the relationship with the teacher became the significant motivator rather than the rewards.

Systems dependent on rewards have been rightly criticized as encouraging people to be externally rather than internally motivated. But the right reward, offered at the right time, can be the catalyst for a huge step in personal growth.

Conclusion

As we grow in understanding of the nuances of consciousness, we learn how to use the appropriate motivation for an individual or group, depending on their Specific Gravity. Helping others grow by motivating them to raise their own energy is becoming more and more common. Rigid forms and dogmatic rules are the way of the past. Instead, we must use our powers of discrimination and intuition to discover what is helpful in each individual situation.

The goal in using the principles of Progressive Development should never be to train others to do your will, but rather to help them overcome resistance that is preventing them from achieving their own goals and using their own willpower. Another way to look at it, is that it is the *dharma* (right action) of the teacher or parent to liberate the student's essence so that energy can express in the highest way possible.

By following the principles of this fifth key, you will find that much conflict and tension between you and those you are responsible for will dissolve. The energy will flow more easily because of your understanding of how to work with it. You will be less attached to the outcomes and more interested in watching the flows of energy play out as you develop your skills to be a positive influence.

CHAPTER 6

Redirect Energy to a Higher Level

Key # 6: Redirect the energy to a higher level rather than trying to suppress it.

Corollary: When the energy is off, blocking it never works in the long run: redirect it instead.

No matter what our goals, success in life depends on being able to generate and sustain energetic effort. Energy can be controlled or undirected. Sometimes we may see a person's overactive energy as negative, but energy, like water, is neutral; it can be used to create and sustain, or to tear down and cause chaos. Some teachers may see an overactive or over-expressive child as a problem. The Education for Life teacher sees this child as having potential once they learn to direct and control their flow of energy. You can dig a new channel for a stream but you cannot create moving water!

When people get agitated or restless, it is tempting to try to bring them back to focus by clamping down and suppressing their energy. However, if this works at all, it is only short-term. It is like putting the lid on a boiling pot of rice; it works only for a while. Eventually, the pot will boil over—or in the case of a student, they may get so discouraged that they shut down or even become antagonistic.

We always want to support energetic enthusiasm in others. But what do we do when the energy is going in a direction that is not positive? Do not repress anyone's energy if it can be avoided. As Einstein said, "Energy cannot be created or destroyed, it can only be changed from one form to another." We need to use our intuition and creativity to discover how we can help others redirect their energy into a more constructive channel.

Whatever the "off" energy is that the child is exhibiting, rather than thinking, "How can I stop it?"—think, "What would this energy look like if it were being expressed at a higher level?"

Let me give you an example. If you have kids who are interested in war and weapons, instead of forbidding this kind of play (which can only drive the interest underground where it becomes even more interesting to them), why not tell stories of how great heroes have fought *for* others, sacrificing themselves to save others? Or create a scenario where they are rescuing the "little kids" when the "monsters" come for them. Suddenly, they are seeing themselves as heroes rather than attackers. It will subtly change their play as they consider saving others, and not just winning.

Once on a field trip to the wonderful High Desert Museum in Oregon, I saw a preteen run up to a telescope and grab it. He never even looked through it to see what might be revealed; instead, he pretended it was a semiautomatic weapon and with sound effects began pretend shooting.

Play like this horrifies some adults, but it will occur in a society where so much entertainment is violent. Even children whose parents do not let them see violent media will pick this up from other children.

Rather than stopping children when they pretend violence, help them uplift their thoughts to the next higher level of consciousness. Do not go too far; should you tell the children to quit and to play a cooperative game, you will be asking them to reach higher than their grasp at that moment. If you ask, "Who are you protecting? Can you save them?" it can reframe their energy. The next few days, you can tell them stories of those who have risked their lives for others, both legendary — a Robin Hood — and factual — Clara Barton. Stories of heroes who risk death to save others or to defend a principle *can* be inspiring and magnetic.

Peggy Dietz, a direct disciple of the Indian teacher Paramhansa Yogananda, told a few friends and me a wonderful story. She said there was a little boy in one of the householder families living at Mount Washington, the estate where Yogananda's headquarters was located. A woman who also lived there came to Yogananda and indignantly asked him whether he knew that this child was playing with a toy gun. She demanded that he put a stop to such unspiritual behavior! Yogananda assured her he would take care of it.

That night at dinner when the little boy entered the dining room, Yogananda, making sure first that the offended lady was listening, exclaimed loudly to the boy, "Hello, Johnny. Come here and tell me about your day. I heard that you have been defending us all from evil people. Keep up the good work!" Peggy giggled and laughed when she told us this story.

The same principle applies to adults, of course. Say you have an employee who loves to gossip about others, causing negativity. Can you have them be responsible for collecting some positive news or accomplishments about each employee (either personal or professional) for a monthly in-house newsletter? Directing their curiosity and interest in others to an uplifting purpose could help enormously.

With either adults or children, it is important that you not make them feel "wrong," but that you recognize they are struggling to direct their energy well. As a leader, you can provide an opportunity for them to make their next step in growth.

Letting Energy Flow

Have you ever had a "class clown" in your group? If so, you know how they love to interrupt, take the attention of the class from the teacher, and generally divert others from what they are doing. Yet, they can be very magnetic and amusing. If they interfere with your agenda and lead your class astray, realize that they have potential for leadership or at least impact. A teacher or leader needs to find a way to get this person on their side as an ally, not as a "teacher's pet," but as a positive influence on others.

It is so tempting to clamp down hard on constant interruptions, but a wise teacher strives to help these students learn self-control and still be themselves.

This means, laughing along with everyone when they make a clever joke, but asking them to save the jokes to the end of class when you will give them the stage. Then you have to follow through and end class a few minutes early and let them get up in front of the class and clown around (within acceptable guidelines). When I have given this type of student class time to entertain occasionally, almost always they gradually start to work with me and control their tendency to grab the class's attention at the wrong time.

Some kids may come to realize they are not all that funny, and stop being silly; others will start refining their little "acts" and actually develop their skill for making others laugh. But whatever happens, it works best if you accept and appreciate the energy of that student and help them channel it. If a teacher tries to completely suppress a creative student's natural energy, it can lead to resentment, rebellion, and/or that student completely disengaging from school. The same thing can happen at home.

It is really helpful for parents, too, to do their best to see kids' energy not as something difficult or disturbing. Remember, it is easier to tame a puppy than to breathe life into an old dog! Of course, this does not mean that the parent ignores impolite or out-of-control behavior, but patiently gives their children acceptable channels for expression. Some of those channels might be sports, martial arts, dance, jobs to assist an adult (this works only if they are working with you; it does not work to send them off to work by themselves), positive friends to play with, or challenges to meet.

Small Opportunities to Encourage an Individual's Energy

When a child's energy is "small" and uncertain, you can help them expand by giving them something to do that you are confident is within their range of ability. Even the smallest of helpful actions can activate a child's energy. For example, when you see a child is holding back from participating, you can ask them to bring you a book from the shelf, or to sharpen a pencil, or turn on some music. Often, another child who exudes enthusiasm will jump up and try to do it because the shy child may be a bit slow to get started. You can say, "Thanks for your willingness to help, but I asked _____ to help this time. You can be helpful by letting others have their turn."

Adults, in their desire to be loving, can sometimes unwittingly discourage children from engaging. Once a mom was visiting my office with her nine-year-old daughter. The girl answered every question I asked in shy monosyllables, but the mom answered *for* her at length. It was apparent the girl didn't need to talk as long as her mom was around. I noticed someone right outside my office struggling to open a door and said to the daughter, who was sitting near the door, "Annie, would you mind opening the door for that little boy?" She turned, saw the child, smiled, and started to get up to help. But before she could get to the door of the office, her mother jumped up and passed her saying, "I'll do it!" and opened the door. Annie, sank back into her chair, silent.

This well-intentioned mother probably thought she was being of service to her daughter, but actually she was depriving her of her ability to access her own energy, and experience her own ability to connect.

Redirecting to a Higher Level

Some kids may get into a habit of criticism to make themselves feel better: "Too bad you're so slow you never finish before lunch;" "Your nose is too big for your face;" or "I don't want you on my team!" It can be challenging for students to avoid sarcasm (at least, in American culture where we are expected to be able to take teasing good-naturedly). But when does affectionate teasing cross over the line into being hurtful? It is so easy for thirteen-year-olds to cross over that line.

I know a middle-school teacher, Carol, who had a rule against sarcasm and put-downs in order to sustain a supportive classroom atmosphere. Now, how did Carol enforce this rule? Did she punish the rule-breaker by denying them recess or giving them a detention? No!! If she heard anyone put down another student, she stopped the class (showing she valued kindness above academic content) and required that the culprit say something positive about the person they just insulted. They had to stop and think of a positive trait or real gesture that person had made to recognize and appreciate, not just a vague, "She's nice." Not only that: then the critical person has to stand up and say one positive about *themselves* to the class!

For the students, this last part was awkward and would result in a lot of good-natured laughter by the rest of the class at their predicament. The perpetrator would usually end up laughing at themselves too, and the negativity would be completely broken. Carol's clever tactic drastically reduced the incidents of inappropriate teasing, and if it did occur, the result would lighten the energy of the whole class.

Is there an objective scale that can help us perceive what is the next step, or higher level of growth in an emotional, social, or spiritual sense? Yes, there is. Simply stated, any experience that helps us become more expansive—more aware of others and more able to see things from others' point of view—is taking us toward maturity. And any experience that causes us to be more contractive, more disinterested in anything outside of our needs and wants, is moving us away from the state of consciousness that brings joy, contentment, and peace of mind. So, you can see that telling children who are pretending to use weapons that they must stop and play a peaceful game will probably result in resentment, not inner peace. At least lifting their minds up to think of protecting others helps them to expand beyond the thought of just being the victor.

When you understand and can recognize levels of Specific Gravity, described in chapter five, it will become easier to see how you can help a child or a group move to a more expansive place, whether that be an Ego-active or a Light level. It is always best to use a motivation that helps raise a person's consciousness to the next level. It is so easy to lose our patience and say, "You better do this or else _____." (For example, you'll have to write sentences! You'll lose your phone privileges! You'll have to stay after school!) This is using consequences as a motivation, which really only works with Heavy energy. Remember, it is best to get the Heavy person moving: "Action is the answer." For the Ego-active, a reward will be much more effective: "After you do this, you can . . . have five minutes extra at recess, watch a half-hour of TV, or play a card game with me."

A Personal Account

In the tenth grade I was in a geometry class with two of my best friends. One was a math brain; one very social. For some reason, I liked geometry and proofs and understood geometry easily (unlike algebra). The three of us sat near each other and chatted and passed notes quite a bit. Every couple of weeks, Ms. Lawson (bless her, wherever she is) would reprimand us and raise her voice and scold us. Once, she was so frustrated with me that she completed a very long proof, erased it, and then turned to me and told me to repeat the whole thing. I did word for word; it was sort of a power play on her part, and unfortunately, I "won" that round. After each time she raised her voice with us, we would be quiet for a week or two until we gave into temptation again. (Don't ask me why she didn't just rearrange the seating.)

Finally, one January day, she had enough, and outraged, she told the three of us we would be staying after school. We were good students and not the type to be offhand about staying after school. I was not afraid, but I was a bit worried about what consequence she was going to give us.

But when we came to her classroom, she did not seem angry. She had us sit in a circle and she spoke to us honestly about how difficult we were making it for her as a teacher. I felt mildly guilty about that. And then she said we were holding back the students in the class who were not as quick as we were in geometry and interfering with their learning. In my egocentric reality, I had never recognized this obvious fact, and I was absolutely *mortified*. I could not believe I had not noticed this. None of us would have deliberately prevented anyone from learning, and we meekly apologized.

My new awareness of the needs of others in the class changed my behavior immediately. From that day until the day we got our yearbooks in May, Ms. Lawson never had to scold us again (signing the yearbooks got us in trouble one last time). I am grateful she talked to us so honestly, rather than punishing us (which would not have helped me rise above that little vortex of self-centered energy). Whether or not she knew what she was doing, her treating us as though we had Light energy (interest in helping others), brought us up to that level.

It is axiomatic, surely, that our children's upbringing ought to be progressive, in the sense of leading them somewhere. Where then should it lead? . . . Isn't the attainment of maturity what growing up is really all about?

Maturity is the ability to relate appro-
priately to other realties than one's
own. Maturity is a continuous — even
a never-ending — process.

J. DONALD WALTERS, *Education for Life*

CHAPTER 7

Be For Something, Not Against Anything

Key 7: It's better to be for something than against anything.

Corollary: Focus your attention in the direction you want to go rather than opposing those who threaten progress toward your goal.

How do we muster our energy in the face of those who oppose us? Have you ever felt that one of your children or students seemed to take issue with everything you said and was determined to oppose whatever course you proposed? Or maybe this has been the case with a colleague or family member. While there is a place for attempting to "win" against such opposition when a principle is involved, in general, opposing is not as effective as creating a positive energy flow. "Rather than spending all your energy trying to win over those who oppose you," Swami Kriyananda has said, speaking of how to be an effective leader, "give your energy to those who are with you. Generally speaking, negativity has little cohesive power compared to the magnetism generated by those who put out positive energy, and who set good examples." (As quoted by Asha Praver in *Swami Kriyananda: As We Have Known Him.*)

An Unusual Conflict Resolution

Idaho's Sun Valley ski resort opened in 1935. In the 1980's, partly fueled by its popularity with Hollywood and high-tech types, the area around the valley, including nearby Ketchum, Idaho, was swept up by a yuppie real estate boom. High-end retirement homes, condominiums, and golf courses attracted urbanites looking to escape the confines of the city. The surrounding area was still rural in character, its economy based on ranching of sheep and cattle. For many years ranchers had moved their herds through the valley a couple of times a year, to higher elevations for grazing in the spring and back to the valleys in autumn.

However, the newer residents objected to livestock disrupting traffic and crossing lawns. As one rancher put it, "It wasn't part of the real estate agreement that sheep would go by and trample the tulips." Out-numbered by the new residents, rural residents were outraged at the criticism of their long-standing way of life. The debate between advocates of the two different cultures seemed unresolvable.

Then someone formed a brilliant idea. New residents are complaining about the livestock? Why not make a festival out of moving the livestock in order to celebrate and educate everyone about the area traditions? They gave the event a snappy name, "Trailing of the Sheep Festival," making it into a major local event with music and refreshments and invited everyone! The schedule of the round-ups and sheep drives were advertised heavily, so that those who wished to avoid the commotion could. Everyone else could attend and witness an aspect of the local economy and culture about which they previously knew little. The festival was an outstanding success.

Fast forward to the present: the festival lasts three days every October, and includes dancing, bagpiping, wool and craft sales, poetry, storytelling, and dog trials — and, of course, the sheep parade! Instead of being a nuisance, the sheep round-ups have become a celebrated part of the Sun Valley/Ketchum culture, an opportunity for community-building, and a boost to the local economy.

Dealing with Discontent

In the early years of our Living Wisdom School, a couple of parents grew critical and fault-finding. Not all of their complaints were unfounded; our staff was on a steep learning curve. We resolved all of the issues that we could, but still, the carping spirit was getting a foothold. We needed to address it before it grew stronger. Someone suggested a meeting with the parents, but I felt that defending

> Sometimes the ones who are against you will forcefully attack you or your position. In those cases, the best response is usually to give the opposition nothing to oppose.
>
> CHRIS ST. HILAIRE,
> *27 Powers of Persuasion*

ourselves would not be helpful. Coming from a position of self-justification is not a position of strength.

Beware of meetings to discuss people's antagonism over what you are doing! Sometimes they may be unavoidable, but, in general, people do not change their point of view because of reasoned arguments. People are emotionally attached to their opinions. What works better than debate? Creating a positive, magnetic flow of energy that may attract their interest, or at least weaken their negativity. Energy is more powerful than words.

Our response was to create and offer a Saturday workshop on the principles of the Education for Life system. Attending parents were swept up in the fun and action, creating a positive atmosphere of shared understanding. They got a bigger picture of the ideals towards which we were striving, and gained appreciation for our teachers. It was good for the staff, too, as they were required to study and refine their understanding to lead the seminar.

Most of the negativity dissipated. The criticism that felt so dire served to create an opportunity for us to generate a stronger flow toward our vision and our mission. Someone once said in front of Swami Kriyananda, "No good deed goes unpunished." Swami replied, "That's not quite right. No good deed goes unchallenged." Do not be surprised, when you are putting your heart and soul into something positive, if someone complains or criticizes. Keep your concentration on your goal, and, if necessary, put out even more positive energy to magnetize your cause.

In the Classroom

One of the most inspired examples I know of this principle was Nitai Deranja's handling of an outbreak of stealing in the classroom. One would think stealing would definitely be something to fight against! A student complained that an item had been taken from a girl's lunch. The next day, food was missing from someone else's lunch. "Everyone began to suspect that someone was stealing food. Quickly the tone of the class deteriorated as children began trying to find out the thief's identity. . . ." (Michael Nitai Deranja, *For Goodness' Sake*). Nitai's response was unconventional: He asked everyone to bring an extra treat from home and secretly slip it into someone else's lunchbox. They did this for a whole week.

"The tone of the class changed dramatically. Instead of seeing one another as potential thieves, now everyone became a possible benefactor." (Deranja) The thefts stopped and the students experienced how sharing brought harmony. In this case, they did discuss how different the class felt and how much more fun it was when everyone not only trusted each other, but gave to each other. Imagine how different the atmosphere of the classroom would have been if he had come down heavy-handed, eventually finding the culprit and giving them a consequence.

Matthew was the oldest child in a blended fourth through sixth-grade classroom. He had a quick brain and was a social leader. Matthew loved sharing the games and routines from the previous year; he was good at them; plus, he enjoyed being the center of attention. As the year went on, however, his leadership, began to have a negative edge. For example, if a mental game he liked to play proved too difficult for some of the class, he became superior and sarcastic.

Because he was such a quick thinker and an impulsive person, it was hard for Matthew to wait for his teacher to finish instructions before jumping in with his own ideas. If he did not like an assignment or boundary that the teacher set, instead of accepting it, he complained vociferously, which caused others in the class to also object. They were simply following their peer leader.

Because Matthew was frustrated, he was not doing the excellent work of which he was capable. His teacher rightly tried to show him the discipline of taking and completing steps toward a goal, but he was too impatient. When the teacher told him more than once or twice that what he was doing was disruptive, Matthew's opposition grew.

We needed to find a channel where his positive energy could flow. Then that positive energy flow would influence other areas of his life as well. In this case, we all noticed that Matthew, while impatient with classmates, showed a great deal of interest and kindness with much younger children—the preschoolers and kindergartners. I requested that the preschool teacher ask whether Matthew could come help one day a week.

Matthew loved the idea of getting out of class to be a helper—it made him feel special and privileged. The preschool teacher warmly included him, and Matthew was wonderful with the three-year-olds. After only a couple of weeks, Matthew had become more cooperative in class, and his defiant energy transformed!

It may seem counterintuitive to allow a student who isn't finishing all of their work to leave the class for a couple of hours a week. However, if you revisit the key and corollary of the chapter, then it makes sense. By putting this student in a position that brought out his heart qualities and helpfulness, his positive energy returned and infused the rest of his time at school. The power struggle between him and the teacher died down because his energy had a positive outlet.

If you reinforce an adversarial energy by fighting against it, you may lose, or you may win. But even if you win, you will expend resources and leave people with resentment. That makes it a hollow victory, to say the least. On the other hand, if you create another magnetic flow of energy, it may very well solve the problem and expand possibilities. Solutions exist when people are open and creative enough to look for them.

The Cosmic Vibration is beyond duality; therefore, in its reality, there's no opposite or opposition. In its consciousness, there is no myself against another—but myself as all others.

JOSEPH BHARAT CORNELL, *AUM: The Melody of Love*

CHAPTER 8

Change Directions with Creativity and Fun

Key 8: When the energy is "off," just do something to change its direction.

Corollary: Let creativity and intuition be your guides to change the direction of the energy when needed.

"I began to realize that an intuitive understanding and consciousness was more significant than abstract thinking and intellectual logical analysis...."

STEVE JOBS

Sometimes the motivational techniques suggested in Chapter Five will work perfectly for you. At other times, when you do not have the time or space to ponder what to do, you need some tools in your belt to change things quickly. You already know that creating a different energy flow is the best answer because energy is more powerful than words, even reasonable words, but how? There are many small things that can ·be the solution—even something as simple as having the group get up and get a drink of water. Use your intuition; *just do something different than what you are doing right now!*

Quick Fixes and the Talking Trash Can

When children are "off," uncooperative, negative, or unwilling, often all that is needed is a quick change of pace to break through that negativity. You really do not have to understand all the principles in the book to effectively "flip the switch." Once the energy changes, the natural energy of the group begins to flow again and problems simply dissolve.

A change in the energy can happen in an instant. It can be done with a joke, a playful game, or turning on some music. I have seen teachers change the energy of their class from distracted and scattered to focused and attentive just by suddenly starting to speak in an accent, singing instructions, turning off the lights, or having the kids stand up and spin around three times.

Years before I conceived of this book, I thought I wanted to share all of the ways I had discovered to "change the energy." In my mind, I called it "101 Ways to Change the Energy," and I started a list, in hopes that other teachers, recreation directors, Sunday School leaders, camp counselors, parents putting on birthday parties, would find some of these techniques helpful in keeping the flow of energy smooth in their groups. In Appendix Three of this book, I have included many of them, but let me suggest a few right here just to start your own creative juices going.

Do not be afraid to look foolish! It is important that whatever you do, it comes from your *own* inspiration, and not merely imitating someone else. Once a specialty teacher who was having some problems with inattention in her class observed a class I taught. I love to play Simon Says with the kids (the way we play is no one is ever out; if they miss, we laugh and just go on) and have practiced quick instructions and ways to fool them. It was fun and brought the kids' energy and attention up. However, I noticed that when the specialty teacher tried the same thing, it fell completely flat and the kids got even more scattered. She went away saying, "That doesn't work." What would have worked was for her to choose and practice her own games and attention-grabbing strategies, activities she was enthusiastic about.

> Never under-estimate the importance of fun to the over-all teaching process. It is often during the moments of lightness, when the mind is diverted, that the most fundamental lessons are absorbed.
>
> J. Donald Walters,
> *Education for Life*

Tim, my co-teacher, and I had a fun class that involved lots of paper-cutting, and we were all picking up scraps. The students' energy was lagging; they were playing more than cleaning up. I announced, "We can go out for recess just as soon as all the scraps are in the trash," but not much was happening. I noticed in one corner a few kids were gathering around the trash can giggling. More kids started picking up trash and heading for that corner. Coming closer, I saw that Tim had drawn two eyes on his forefinger. With thumb and forefinger pinched together, the gap in the middle was a mouth saying, "Feed me. Please feed me." When a child inserted a scrap of paper, the "mouth" made satisfied noises. Completely bypassing any analysis of the Law of Motivation, Tim's creativity and humor completely outstripped my attempts to motivate! Humor and fun lift the energy, and keep it light enough to move freely and make the classroom ever new.

Works with Adults Too

The staff of a fundraising project I was working on had a regular early morning meeting to update each other on our progress and hash out problems. While we shared an overall consensus about the project, small decisions could hang us up. One morning we were struggling with a dispute about the best course to take.

Each side was sure that their opinion was correct, and while respectful, no one would concede. Every single person had spoken. I noticed most of us were looking at the floor, frowning. "Uh, oh," I thought, "This is getting bad; we need to change this heavy energy."

Just as I had that thought, the leader stood up and exclaimed, "Let's take a tea and coffee break!" With relief, we got up to get refreshments and began socializing. Although we were not addressing the problem head on, we *were addressing the energy*; moments before we were exasperated, worn down, and unwilling to step outside our own views. Now we were moving around, chatting, eating and drinking—completely taking us out of the negative vortex of energy.

> The significant problems we face cannot be solved by the same level of thinking that created them.
>
> ALBERT EINSTEIN

Sure enough, when the chair called us back to order in eight or ten minutes, someone immediately raised her hand and suggested a compromise that would allow us to move ahead without anyone's position being ignored. The solution arose because our collective state of mind had changed—not because we reasoned our way to it.

Changing the Energy Before Discussing

Recess was over. The first children to return to the classroom were breathless and flushed with exertion, but their faces weren't the smiling faces of children who just had a good recess. Clearly, the playground time hadn't gone so well.

Several children rushed up to me, appeal in their eyes.

"The fifth-graders were mean to us. They wouldn't let us on the swings!"

"What did you do about it?"

"We told them they had to take turns and we got in line, but then they just pushed in ahead of us!"

The fifth-graders, walking in the door and hearing the fourth-graders' complaints, raised their voices to defend themselves, "That's not true! You guys came out and cut in line in front of us and only two of us had even gotten a turn. And then you threw sticks at everybody on the swings and called us names!"

As the two groups confronted each other, I slipped away to start some music. Bach, Mozart, music from Crystal Clarity—any of these would have been useful—but I saw that "I, Omar" was already in the player, so I turned it on and rejoined the group.

"I want everyone to get your water bottle, and sit down, and drink some before we discuss this." In their overheated, agitated states, their need for water was evident.

"We need to discuss what happened and help everyone to resolve this situation, but first let's cool off. I'm going to return your crossword puzzles from yesterday, while you relax in silence."

By this time, the music had begun to calm the students and the water to cool them and restore balance. Their emotions having been roused, they craved a quiet time to pull back, but their egos could not do this on their own; they needed an adult's help. As they drank and the music played, I noticed that their faces had lost their intense agitation and their breathing calmed. Only one or two still look disgruntled.

"Today I planned for us to continue working on our research projects or our drawings of bird feet," I remarked.

A hand raised, "Can I use markers instead of colored pencils to color my drawings?"

Another hand: "Can I use the computer to find a photo of an osprey?"

"Yes, to both," I replied. "But first!, don't we need to talk about what happened at recess?"

"No, I want to work on my project!" she said. Others were already getting out their drawings and their notes.

Only two or three students who were directly involved in the incident still wished to talk it out. Because their emotions were so much calmer and they were now in a safe environment, they were willing to listen as well as air their own complaints. Most of the children had already let go of their anger and were ready to move on.

There are many tools and techniques to change the energy of a class, but *music* is one of the strongest and best tools to create positive energy. Music works on a vibrational level to change the consciousness. Even unconsciously listening to calming music, the students' bodies and breath relax, which then calms their emotions and mental agitation.

Notice that we did not try to resolve things by talking first, I just did several things to shift their energy so they were able to address the issue from a different consciousness. The next crisis, I might ask the children themselves, "What would be a good thing to do to help us become calmer before we talk about this?" This would help them develop the awareness and the skills to help themselves on an energy level before tackling an issue with words.

Compose Yourself

Often when teachers and parents struggle with behavior problems, they spend a lot of time talking with the child or children (over and over) about how their behavior should change. A first-year teacher had a disastrous Physical Education class where the children clowned around and constantly distracted each other from listening to the game directions. They could not play without the instructions, so they got upset with each other.

Exasperated, the teacher took them inside and spent half an hour scolding them and trying to reason with them about what they had done and what they could do differently. Some were angry and others simply felt badly, either because they had no fun or because the teacher was upset. That lecture really did not help the culprits because they were busy mentally defending themselves ("She's too strict;" "We never get to have fun;" "What I did wasn't that bad.") Others were just ready to move on.

Again, whether adults or children, we cannot solve problems at the level at which we created them. The time would have much better been spent just changing the energy. The teacher could have read aloud or had them all draw or read silently while listening to music. Later, after everyone's energy was more harmonious, they could discuss the incident and create solutions from a different state of mind.

When we are in "problem consciousness" our outlook has to change first before we can see any solutions. And this means our own attitude first! We cannot help others until we can uplift our own state of mind. In Becky Bailey's Conscious Discipline model, the very first skill for teachers and parents is Composure. She understands that we cannot deal with the ups and downs of others if we are not in a calm state of mind ourselves. Often you will find that a change of your attitude alone will solve the problem, and if not, you are creating the right "energy" (or emotional environment) for the solutions to emerge.

> An important point to be realized, when helping children to achieve fresh insight into the problems they encounter in daily life, is that the intellectual understanding of a problem is not only insufficient, but often is not helpful at all. What is important is that they find themselves moving happily in a new direction, and not that they themselves understand all the reasons for the direction.
>
> J. DONALD WALTERS,
> *Education for Life*

Deeper Changes Needed

Sometimes a group may get into a negative downward spiral for reasons beyond the teacher's control, for example, an emotional upheaval in the children's home lives, the atmosphere of the school as a whole, or a pandemic. The teacher must ask himself first, "What needs are not being met? Are the students bored? Is the work too difficult? Do I vary my approach enough?" and make adjustments. I am in no way recommending ignoring issues that need honest and sympathetic attention. However, sometimes the problem is not dramatic or deep, and the attention just needs to be shifted.

All kids whine and complain occasionally, but sometimes the energy gets so "off" that the little tricks work for a few minutes, but then the class falls back into negativity or even just dullness. A longer-term plan to shift the energy may be needed. An example of something easy to try is to change the seating. If kids are frequently talking and not paying attention to you, rearrange the room. Sometimes it is enough to break up combinations of students who have fallen into a pattern of reinforcing each other's negativity. Warn the children a day ahead of time that the seating will change. You will probably get lots of moaning and complaining for a couple of days, but notice how rearranging the seating changes the dynamics of the class.

I gave an example of this sort of shift in the last chapter, when Nitai Deranja had his students bring in surprises to slip in students' lunch boxes. Our first year of the Ananda Portland school the teachers and I noticed that the children seemed a little "off" or just not as happy to be at school as they were at the beginning of the year. I realized we all needed a lift and suggested a couple of field trips. Wonderful nature parks, children's theater, and pumpkin patches provided plenty of opportunities; and planning the events, learning about what we'd see beforehand, and changing the routine provided just the energy boost the group needed.

Once on a field trip to eastern Oregon, we stayed in two cabins in a state park. A few students played a trick on the other cabin by moving their shoes (left outside the door) around and hiding a few. Of course, that required a retaliatory raid. The kids did not know how or when to stop, and the practical joke energy got out-of-hand quickly with kids becoming angry because they could not find their shoes. The teacher and I had to "lay down the law" about no more shoe-hiding, but resentful feelings lingered. The next day the teacher came up with a brilliant idea. She conspired with the children riding in her car to surprise the kids in the other cabin with a treat to leave on the others' beds that evening. We heard squeals of delight from the other cabin when they discovered their surprises, and any lingering disgruntled emotions just dissipated.

A similar dynamic works within families. When your family is going through a rough patch for whatever reason, consider what might shift the energy and be healing for all of you together. For example, maybe a visit to a favorite relative or a project to work on together (such as cheering up an elderly neighbor who has lost a spouse), or even play a board game together.

Again, it is not that you ignore the reasons for the difficulties, whether relationships or outside pressures or a child's issues at school; definitely accept those difficulties and think about how to improve them. At the same time, balance this with an effort to focus on and increase the flow of positive energy. The more we focus on this positive flow, the more magnetism we have to attract creative, uplifting solutions.

It is important when you are looking for an energy shift that you tune into what is happening and get your own inspiration for action that is congruent with who you and your group are. Talking with a colleague who knows your class and situation can be helpful, if you feel stuck, but also, do your best to seek your own inner guidance. You may be surprised at the answers that come when you heart is open, and your energy is composed.

Modeling Changing Energy to Children

A class of fifth and sixth-graders returned to school from a play at a local so-called children's theater. As the children got out their lunches, I asked, "How was the play?"

A sixth-grader boy's eyes got wide, "Oh, Usha, you wouldn't have liked it," he said.

"I wouldn't?" I studied the children's faces. They all nodded, looking serious. I knew immediately that some of them hadn't liked it either, but in order to avoid appearing "uncool" they were projecting their feelings on me.

"No, you wouldn't," several said.

"Why, was it violent?"

"Kind of," a couple of kids said.

"Not exactly," Hannah struggled for a word, "It was just . . . just . . ."

"Dark," the teacher said.

"Yeah," agreed the kids.

Another girl in the class listlessly played with her lunch box. "I just feel yucky, like I need a shower."

Because their parents and teachers encouraged their sensitivity and provided a safe environment, these children were not afraid to be vulnerable and recognize their heart's repulsion to negative energy that had no uplifting meaning or purpose.

"Well, how can we change our feelings?" I asked, leaping on the opportunity to see if they remembered what we'd discussed in a class we had been teaching them called Brain Gain.

"Drink water?"

"Yes!"

"Run outside?"

"Yes, but we can't do that right this minute."

"Take deep breaths."

"Yes, let's do that. And remember how music can change our mood? Let's sing an uplifting song!" and we launched into a song all the kids knew. Most of them joined in, and soon all were over it and ready to eat lunch.

If you reflect on it, you may discover that too much talking and explaining just teaches children to parrot what you say. Analysis can lead to paralysis! If you really want to effect lasting change, you need to help them *experience* a change in energy. We learn from *experience* — a basic principle of Education for Life — much better than from what we merely hear about. There are adults in their mid-thirties and forties now who attended Education for Life Living Wisdom Schools. I see in their work and lives an intuitive understanding of how to create an uplifting environment and keep the energy moving positively. They feel it and act on it in a way that those of us in an older generation can but admire.

Who would kill the song in a child's heart? Instead of explaining the benefits of living harmoniously, why not get the children simply to do whatever will help them to live in harmony with themselves and with others? Action, far more than words, will uplift them into a positive outlook.

J. Donald Walters, *Education for Life*

AFTERWORD

Love is the "Master Key"

The master key to the laws of the universe is love.

Swami Kriyananda, *Religion in the New Age*

Love Affirms the Highest

We had a new teacher in the school who was struggling with her class. She had great ideas and a fun-loving attitude, and I was mystified about the problem. I felt a little bit responsible because I had supported hiring her. Cheryl, (I will call her) complained a great deal about her students, although she clearly adored most of them. At the end of every school year, we had an Awards Day where every student receives an award for a quality or life skill. First-year teachers often find it challenging to come up with the quality and an anecdote to support it, so I volunteered to help her. We started with the students who were easy for her to identify great traits. But when we got to one particular student, a student I knew she had difficulties with, Cheryl could not come

92

up with a single positive thing to say about her. I was stunned. This was an engaging, intelligent girl; there had to be several possibilities of strengths to mention. In fact, I would say that she and one other student were the leaders in the class. One of the difficulties had been that this student was so intel-ligent that she sometimes cor-rected the teacher's errors; had that caused this rift?

I realized that much of the struggle Cheryl had all year with this class was not only that she had not identified something positive she could admire and encourage in each student, but that she had failed to do so with a student who was most influential over all of the class! While it is true that personalities can conflict, it is absolutely necessary for a good teacher to set aside differences and be impersonal in identifying each student's gifts and reflect-ing them back — opening doors of possible development that perhaps neither the teacher nor the student can see at the time.

> Seek to inspire others with faith in their own high potential. Never speak belittling of them when they fall short of your expecta-tions. Your faith in them, or your lack of it, will determine to a great extent the success of your endeavors.
>
> SWAMI KRIYANANDA,
> *Secrets of Life*

When we see the highest aspirations within each soul, we open a door for those aspirations to be realized. As the flow of energy increases through those channels, the energy will increase in the whole person. The weaker aspects of their personality will get energy too, and the willingness to face them and change will grow.

Early in my teaching days, before I understood or could use most of the eight keys, I had a student who had a rather tumultuous childhood because her mother lived on one coast, and her father on the other. She spent one full school year with each alternately, and didn't see the other parent more than once during each year. Sharon was a quite intelligent girl; I enjoyed her mental acuity and her love for reading when I had her as a fifth-grader. Later, when I was her homeroom teacher in ninth-grade, I realized that she was also quite physically inclined. She loved dance, as I found out when we had a little class talent show.

Sharon happened to be visiting friends in the community after her first year at Pitzer College. I was so touched when she sought me out after the annual Awards Day ceremony and Living Wisdom School graduation to say, "I just want you to know that you really made a difference!"

"Oh, Sharon, thank you so much. I am so glad. Tell me what I did that made a difference so I can be sure I do it for other students!"

She thought for a few seconds and replied, "It was that you believed in me; you believed I could do things."

Identifying anyone's gifts and talents does not involve analysis so much as attention and intuition. Tune into each individual deeply. What inspires them? What activities are they engaged in when their energy is focused and they forget themselves? Do not just notice what they are *good* at; what actually feeds them? What makes them experience inner joy?

Magnetism that Draws the Highest

A couple of students and I were giving a teacher from another school a tour of our school. A parent had highly recommended this teacher to me, and I looked forward to meeting her. She was full of personality, and very lively as we showed her around our classrooms. The parent had hinted that she might be interested in moving to a new position, but something vague was holding me back from asking her for an interview. I could see that she would engage the children; what was it I felt uncomfortable about?

Watching the different children respond to her, I realized that she was always the center of attention, chatting and telling stories, but she gave the children little opportunity to talk. Keeping the kids' attention by the power of her personality and magnetism was easy for her, but I did not sense she was really interested in taking the students beyond that. She sold everyone on her own gifts and personality, but did not know how to sell the students on their own gifts and aspirations. She loved the kids, but not in a way of helping them know themselves.

Contrast that to one of my teachers, who was also well-liked by the children (although maybe not with such effusion, which may well burn out). She also told personal stories and shared inspiration, but not in a way that drew the students to herself, but in a way that drew them to consider the high ideals that guided her. Her love for her students was not personal, but rather a commitment to the highest in each child and the desire to understand them so she could help them to develop their own gifts.

One year, for her birthday, her class secretly (a few parents knew, but the teacher and I did not) hatched a plan to memorize part of Martin Luther King Jr.'s "I Have a Dream" speech to recite for her. They alerted me that morning so I could be part of honoring her. The sight and sound of these sixth-graders standing together and reciting gave me chills.

> Let us not wallow in the valley of despair, I say to you today, my friends. I have a dream that my four little children will one day live in a nation where they will not be judged by the color of their skin but by the content of their character. I have a dream today.
>
> So even though we face the difficulties of today and tomorrow, I still have a dream. It is a dream deeply rooted in the American dream. I have a dream that one day this nation will rise up and live out the true meaning of its creed: We hold these truths to be self-evident, that all men are created equal. . . .

These calm and engaged students exuded love and joy, both for their teacher and for the ideals she had pointed them toward. They were self-forgetful and united in their purpose. They were definitely in Light Specific Gravity, blossoming with beautiful soul qualities that this teacher's love had inspired in them.

In 1993, the author of *Education for Life* generously agreed to be interviewed for a promotional video. At one point he made a remark that I had never heard him put exactly in that way before. He said, "A good teacher must love his subject!" He paused, and then continued, "Or in the case of a teacher of young children, must love childhood itself!" "Love childhood itself"—what a concept.

As I have observed excellent teachers through the years, I have seen that to be so true. In fact, I would say it goes beyond loving childhood—right up through early adolescence. Love is incredibly powerful whether it is for a phase of life, the arts, sports, an academic subject, or each other.

Love All Aspects

The magnetism of love of one's subject and the enthusiasm that love generates attracts students and sometimes changes their lives as life-long interests are ignited. LOVE enters into education in many ways. Yes, this is a book about energy; however, I do not want to leave you with the idea that I think that understanding energy and motivation is the be-all-end-all of wisdom! No. I believe the number one secret to teaching and helping others is LOVE. When you consciously become a channel for love to each person, the heart opens and intuitions and opportunities flow in. It is almost as if the universe sees an opening for love and does everything to assist.

I am not speaking about a *personal* love that involves attachment and the desire to be loved back, but an *impersonal* love that might be described as loving everyone as a child of God (or a manifestation of the divine, since we are talking about being impersonal!). This kind of love wishes the best for each individual and perceives gifts or inclinations in each person that could blossom. When we wish someone well, whether child or co-worker, spouse or neighbor, when we genuinely see their strengths, and when we strive to give them opportunities to grow, a person knows this intuitively. They begin to relax, to trust you, and to open up, and to want to fulfill your belief in their potential. The power of this kind of mutual respect and love between teacher and student, parent and child, or any two people is unfathomable. It is an opportunity to experience the sacred on earth and can bring so much joy.

It is not necessary to use words to encourage others, although words can be very powerful. Discover the power of your positive regard, sweet smiles that include the eyes, a gentle touch on the arm or shoulder and the power of simple good will.

When you cannot feel that love because you are tired, exasperated, angry or disappointed, remember that Love exists and can flow through you when you ask. Sometimes you have to change your state of consciousness to tune into it, but you do not have to generate it yourself because it exists. You can choose to be around those people and situations who inspire it in you.

I like the slogan, "Be the reason someone smiles today." What a worthy goal! But we can take that sentiment so much deeper and affect others much more powerfully. Be the reason today that someone senses their own inner potential to go beyond the little boundaries of self-definition that currently bind them. Often, this may be difficult as we deal with life's daily challenges and conflicts, and my advice does not mean to ignore where others currently are in their continuum of progressive development, but absolutely to accept where they are. It means to look for ways to encourage them on their *next* step to growth (not some future ideal). It is necessary to feel sensitively where they are ready to mature so you can provide opportunities they can grasp.

It is said that energy has its own intelligence. My mind cannot really understand this, and yet, I have experienced it. It appears that we live in a fixed physical universe, but everything changes constantly, controlled by the energy behind what we see. Tuning into that reality, and especially to loving all as manifestations of the divine, the heart opens, and there is space for solutions to arise. Once you start to live with awareness of the constant flux of flowing energy, you begin to let go of attachments to things as you want them to be. In this lack of attachment, there is room for much more freedom and joy.

In this book, I have shared with you eight key concepts of working with energy that helped me become a better colleague, friend, teacher, and principal. If you are just beginning the journey of seeing everything as energy, not form, eight principles are a lot to take in all at once. But working with any one of the keys will lead you to greater insights and new skills. Just choose one that resonates with you and start practicing. Remember, "Action is the answer!"

It has been my privilege to work with wonderful parents, teachers, and educators who have these attitudes and who taught me so much about unselfishness, unconditional love, and how to have a sense of humor about the setbacks! My wish for you is that you will also find a like-minded community of those who are willing to risk letting go of old forms and who are willing to work sensitively with energy. And most importantly, with LOVE. From my experience, I can predict that you will discover expansion and joy as you let go of rigidity and embrace flows of positive energy.

Love is patient, love is kind. It does not envy, it does not boast, it is not proud. It does not dishonor others, it is not self-seeking, it is not easily angered, it keeps no record of wrongs. Love always protects, always trusts, always hopes, always perseveres.

I CORINTHIANS 13:4-6, 7

APPENDIX ONE

Using the Appropriate Motivation

What Specific Gravity Level (Heavy, Ego-active, Light) would each statement most likely motivate?

1. If you don't quit that right now, I'll make you get out of the car.

2. Please help me clean up, so grandma will enjoy her visit more.

3. Put all the toys away and straighten the shoes while I vacuum, and then I will read you a story.

4. Stop hitting your brother or you'll have to go to your room.

5. Let's pick some flowers and take them to our neighbor.

6. If you bring your coat home every day this week, I will buy the new shoes you want.

7. If you don't go to bed right now, you are not going to get any new shoes.

8. Your mother and I work hard to buy us all clothes. Can you make more of an effort to bring home everything you wore to school?

The answers are in Appendix Four.

APPENDIX TWO

Activities that Change the Energy!

AWAKEN ENTHUSIASM

1. Run around the building several times
2. Challenges
   In 30 seconds, how many times can you...?
   Do three math problems in 2 minutes, etc.
   Name three things (choose appropriate item/
   category, e.g. colors, animals, months)
3. Play lively music and lead some dance moves or
   calisthenics
4. Tennis balls or beanbags: toss up and spin
   around and catch; bounce twice and catch; other
   challenges
5. Balloons: play music; two people per balloon
   keep the balloon from touching the floor with
   different body parts called out (little finger, el-
   bow, forehead, left foot, and so on)
6. Leader wears a costume to class
7. Juggle or perform some other feat and challenge
   kids to do it
8. Bring in homemade treats or fruit to share, such
   as watermelon or berries
9. Change your voice or diction (for example, to a
   ballpark announcer, or a country-western singer)

10. Any energizer or icebreaker video you find and like
11. Energization Exercises

FOCUS ATTENTION

1. Simon Says (with no one being "out")
2. Play music—Baroque or other calming music
3. Balance feats
     book placed on head
     carry bell without ringing it
     potato on spoon
     dried beans on a table knife
     stand on one foot and extend the other
        backwards
4. Skip counting/mental math
5. Concentration challenges with props—tennis balls, beanbags, card decks
6. Silent follow-the-leader, sign language, pantomime
7. Work in silence
8. Practice writing letters in the air
9. Games (button on a string, Bird, Beast, Fish)
10. Great read-alouds
11. Sing instructions
12. Time them on anything
13. Breathing exercises
14. Yoga postures or Tai Chi
15. Sing a round or a song with hand motions
16. Cook's Hook-up
17. Wiggle and Stop (see "I Am Master of Myself; I Am Connected to All" from *Education for Life*)

SHARE INSPIRATION

This can be with the whole group, a small group, a partner, or individually with the teacher or parent.

1. Art
2. Music
3. Dance
4. Writing
5. Circle sharing
   - Tell the most fun thing that happened.
   - Share one thing you learned (or were reminded of).
   - Share how you felt when _____ .
   - Give a statement of appreciation to someone else in the group.
6. Perform a skit.
7. Teach someone else what we have learned.
8. Share a meal together.
9. Hold hands and sing a song together.
10. Be in silence and bless each other.
11. Healing prayers for others.

VARIABLE

These are examples of when the energy of the class or group will definitely change; it is hard to predict for sure how.

1. A new person joins the group
2. A pet visits the class
3. Fire alarm bell rings
4. It starts to snow

5. Turn off the lights and light a candle
6. Move the class to a new location
7. Lie down on the grass and look at the sky
8. Play music
9. Go outside

APPENDIX THREE

Music to Change the Energy

ACTIVATING

She'll Be Comin' Round the Mountain
If You're Happy and You Know It
When the Saints Go Marchin' In
Hokey Pokey
Jingle Bells
Zip a Dee Doo Dah
Red, Red Robin
Manana
Some Bluegrass, some soft rock
Chants such as "Dance with Me"

CALMING

Home on the Range
Kumbaya
Michael, Row the Boat Ashore
We Shall Overcome
Silent Night
Cello and Flute for Relaxation
Mozart for Relaxation
Most lullabies

Stephen Halpern's music
Baroque music (gentle classical)

FOCUSING

rounds
    Row, Row, Row Your Boat
    Give Me a Light, etc.)
Bingo (B-i-n-g-o)
I'll Tell the World (from *All the World is My Friend*
    songbook)
Little Cabin in the Woods
Eensy-Weensy Spider (for younger children)
Call and response songs, such as My Aunt Came
    Back
Music for concentration
    such as Baroque music

UPLIFTING

My Favorite Things (from *Sound of Music*)
The Happy Wanderer
A few hymns, such as Battle Hymn of the Republic
Songs on *All the World Is Your Friend*
Chanting
    Gregorian and other spiritual traditions
Crystal Clarity music
Mozart

AGITATING

Some rock music, especially heavy metal,
Some rap
Discordant "modern music"

These selections are examples. If you have questions about a selection, try to be still, listen, and feel. You can learn to identify the effects of different types of music by following this process.

APPENDIX FOUR

Answer Key to Appendix One

1. Heavy (motivated to avoid pain only)

2. Ego-Active (motivated by reward)

3. Light (motivated to seek truth and/or help others)

4. Heavy (motivated to avoid pain only)

5. Ego-Active (motivated by reward)

6. Heavy (motivated to avoid pain only)

7. Light (motivated to seek truth and/or help others)

8. Ego-Active (motivated by reward)

9. Heavy (motivated to avoid pain only)

10. Light (motivated to seek truth and/or help others)

APPENDIX FIVE

Flow Learning®

Flow Learning® is a model for conducting nature activities developed by International nature educator Joseph Cornell. Noticing that participants in his groups were often not ready to absorb the benefits of the games he created, he learned to begin with activities that grabbed the learners' interest and attention. You can find more details in *Flow Learning: Opening Heart and Spirit Through Nature*, the latest book in the Sharing Nature Book series by Joseph Bharat Cornell, and at sharingnature.com.

Based on the same principles of energy as *Education for Life*, *Flow Learning* is a perfect complement to working with Specific Gravity. *Flow Learning* helps to activate the members of the group who may be in a Heavy or Contractive Ego-active state, and focuses the attention of all the participants. The Flow Learning® system is very effective in the classroom for lesson planning, as well as elsewhere for organizing any group experience, such as meetings, retreats, assemblies and other gatherings. It works for any age.

Four Steps of *Flow Learning®* Explained

Awaken Enthusiasm: This step activates the participants' energy and gets their attention. Attention is the first step for learning or expansion. This step could build on past experiences; it could be a game that involves movement, especially for children. Importantly, it strengthens rapport between the teacher/leader and participants. You know when your activity has succeeded when you see **alertness** in the faces of your audience.

An Awaken Enthusiasm activity for a speech or oral presentation might be to tell a joke and/or a story that is relatable to your audience and gets them to relax and be open to your message. To begin a math class, one might start with a few physical exercises where they have to use math (do 3 times 3 minus 3 jumping jacks, take 100 divided by 4 steps to your left and then 21 steps to your right).

Focus Attention: The second step directs the awakened energy to a common focus. The energy generated by Awaken Enthusiasm becomes calmer but no less strong. Often this step brings concentration into the experience by requiring the individuals to respond in some way. The quality this activity should produce is **receptivity.**

For the Focus Attention activity of a weekend seminar, participants might be paired up and given time for a brief interview of each other. Then one person from each pair introduces themselves and their partner and names one thing they have in common. The entire group repeats their names and that one word for what both like or share requiring the whole group's focus and attention.

When you have solved the problem of controlling the attention of the child, you have solved the entire problem of its education.

MARIA MONTESSORI

Direct Experience: This is the main part of the experience. Too often the leader of a session launches right into this—understandable because it is through experience that we learn— but it is essential that our energy and attention be engaged to benefit from the experience. The quality to look for is **absorption.** If the learning activity is succeeding, the students will be absorbed in it, or "in the flow" as we might say.

This step could be working on a project, practicing a skill, watching a demonstration, or even listening to a magnetic teacher. In a math class, this might be some individuals working on the board, and others working on problems in pairs, and the teacher demonstrating to another group. In a literature class, it might be reading a play aloud, or writing haiku.

Share Inspiration: The final stage involves reflection and sharing with others, both of which reinforce what was learned. Also, this step encourages expansion beyond one's own limited reality. This step could be sharing a project with an adult or another class, expressing the impact of the experience through writing or drawing, or even a celebratory meal together.

The qualities of this step are **clarity and idealism.** An example of this step could be the wrap-up for a week-long Education for Life course where participants share something they learned or observed during the weekend and how they plan to take this example back into their own settings.

SAMPLES OF FLOW LEARNING FORMAT

The following samples will give you an idea of how Flow Learning works, step-by-step in three different contexts.

A Workshop for Teachers on Specific Gravity

Awaken Enthusiasm: Have everyone rate their energy and enthusiasm level on a scale of 1-10. Then throw out balloons, play lively music, and challenge participants to keep the balloons in the air using only their elbows and heads.

Focus Attention: Sit down and rate your energy level now. Why did it change? Raise your hand if it increased. Why did that happen?

Direct Experience: Facilitator teaches Specific Gravity with a talk that includes photos, stories, and more activities such as checklists that help them reflect on Progressive Development.

Share Inspiration: Divide the attendees into groups of three or four and have them share with each other insights they gained about how they might change their approach to handling a classroom challenge based on what they learned today. Let one representative from each group share an insight with everyone.

Committee Meeting

Awaken Enthusiasm: Serve refreshments.
Focus Attention: Look at the agenda and ask for additions.
Direct Experience: Address the agenda.
Share Inspiration: Summarize the actions committed to during the meeting, and ask someone else to share what they were most enthusiastic about or inspired by.

Meditation Practice (Sadhana, Ananda Style)

Awaken Enthusiasm: Energization Exercises
Focus Attention: Prayer and Chanting
Direct Experience: Meditation Techniques
Share Inspiration: Healing Prayer

Flow Learning is Flexible

While Flow Learning *may* be thought of as a lesson plan format, it is much more. It is effective for the structure of an entire unit, for an event such as a parent/student gathering, and even for an entire school year. Try planning your next class or event using Flow

Learning, and you will see how effective it is. Why? Because it works with an understanding of the eight energy keys.

After some experience working with this model, you will find that some activities cover two steps simultaneously. Often an Awaken Enthusiasm activity will also Focus Attention, and two different activities are not necessary. Sometimes the Direct Experience activity is interesting enough to Focus Attention. You may even see that you can skip both first steps and jump right into the Direct Experience if you are working with a group on a project that they are all engaged in and eager to continue.

Strict adherence to this format bypasses the whole point: Is there a flow of energy where the majority of the group are engaged, and are we moving toward expansion? By tuning into this ideal flow of energy for receptivity, you will learn to recognize when an energy shift is needed and why.

APPENDIX SIX

The Eight Keys in Review

Chapter One **Excitement vs. Happiness
(Energy Awareness)**

Key 1: Engaged energy leads to contentment; merely excited energy often ends in disappointment.
Corollary: Seek to be calmly active and actively calm.

- Excitement and happiness are easily confused for each other. Learn to discriminate between the two.
- The ideal mental state to learn new skills is a state of "relaxed alertness"—attentive, but without tension.
- Practice reading the energy of those around you and notice what type of energy leads to what outcomes.
- When you are engaged, that is involved in an activity approaching a point of self-forgetfulness, a flow of energy is created that has its own intelligence.

Chapter 2 **Nurture Enthusiasm**

Key 2: Always nurture enthusiasm: the energy is more important than the details.

Corollary: You can help someone redirect their positive energy, but you cannot generate it for them once it's taken away.

- Recognize the positive flow of energy of others' enthusiasms.
- Affirm the strengths in those around you. This increases the flow of energy, whereas focusing on weaknesses inhibits the flow.
- The right spirit is invaluable. When someone has it, their accomplishments will outstrip their knowledge.

Chapter 3 Getting Unstuck: Action is the Answer!

Key 3: When the energy is "stuck," action is the answer.
Corollary: Almost any action is better than inaction—once the energy starts to flow, the momentum can be turned in the direction you wish to go.

- The bridge from mental dullness to higher awareness is constructed of intense activity of some kind.
- When you are "stuck," unable to take a step in the direction you want to go, find something else to act upon that will start your energy moving.
- Reason and words are not effective when the energy is heavy; just get moving and discuss the issue later.

Chapter 4 **Energy Follows Will**

Key 4: Energy flows where there is willingness.
Corollary: The greater the will, the greater the flow of energy—to lead others, tune into their interests and motivations.

- Practice a willing attitude toward everything that life brings you, and you will have more energy to use toward your goals.
- To motivate others, notice the types of activities and situations that stimulate a positive energy flow for them and provide more opportunities for them in these directions.
- Choices engage our will; to help others follow through, offer some element of choice.

Chapter 5 **I Can't. Why Should I? I Will!
(Progressive Development)**

Key 5: Motivation varies according to the level of energy.
Corollary: You enhance the flow of energy when you use the motivation appropriate for the level of energy.

Specific Gravity	Attitude	Motivated...
Light	I will!	by search for truth and helping others
Ego-Active	Why should I?	by what's in it for me and mine?
Heavy	I can't.	to avoid pain

- Everyone is on a continuum of soul development from contractive self-centeredness to joyful expansion, called Progressive Development.

- When people are unmotivated—unwilling, uncooperative, and negative—we call their energy
  Heavy. They are motivated chiefly by the desire to avoid pain. Consequences (such as, "You
  cannot have a play date unless you turn in all
  your homework") are appropriate when children
  are stuck in this energy. An even better way to
  get them unstuck is to get them moving, *doing*
  anything. *Action is the answer!*
- When individuals can be motivated by their
  desire to obtain something, we call them
  Ego-active. They want something for themselves, whether it's praise, another star on a star
  chart, success, or success for their own children.
  The Ego-active level is energetic, but often restless and not centered.
- When individuals are not thinking of themselves, but are enjoying a process or activity in
  and for itself, they are Light. At this level they
  are motivated to help others (this is likely the
  only time you can say, "Your little sister is unhappy, will you play with her?" and get a positive response) and to seek truth (learn, grow,
  expand).
- Offer others a motivation at least on the level
  of energy they are in, or the next higher level,
  to encourage them to reach upward. If you offer
  a lower motivation, for example a consequence
  when a reward would work, or a reward when
  they would do it for the joy of it, you bring them
  down to a lower level.
- If we force a child to behave at the Light level

when their energy is Heavy, we do them a dis-
service, as they will probably resent the behavior. For example, forcing a child to share his toy
when he is feeling contractive and Heavy may
make him resent sharing.

- These levels represent a continuum, not three
distinct levels. Our own calmness and detach-
ment are key to perceiving where someone is on
the continuum and how we can appeal to them.
- In working with a group, it is most effective to
direct your energy and attention toward those
who are acting from a Light and Expansive
Ego-active level, as their enthusiasm and energy
will in turn motivate others in the group.

Chapter 6 Redirect Energy to a Higher Level

Key 6: Redirect the energy to a higher level rather than
trying to suppress it.
Corollary: When the energy is off, blocking it never works
in the long run—redirect it instead.

- When someone's energy is going in a direction
that is not helpful, do not attempt to suppress it,
but find a way to redirect it into a channel that
is more helpful to what is trying to happen.
- Give others who may hang back or be uncertain
small opportunities to assert their energy in
positive ways to help them experience their own
power.
- Always offer those who are ready an opportunity
to rise to a higher level of awareness by giving
them an option that is just above their current
level of Specific Gravity.

Chapter 7 **Be *For* Something, Not Against Anything**

Key 7: It's better to be for something than against anything.

Corollary: Focus your attention in the direction you want to go rather than opposing those who threaten progress toward your goal.

- When others oppose you, look for avenues to generate positive energy that is stronger than the opposition.
- When students or employees are engaging in non-helpful ways, look for a way to get them involved in a positive energy flow.

Chapter 8 **Change Directions with Creativity and Fun**

Key 8: When the energy is "off," just do something to change its direction.

Corollary: Let creativity and intuition be your guides to change the direction of the energy when needed.

- Develop a repertoire of engaging activities that change the group energy quickly from boredom or distraction to focused attention and engagement.
- When you do not have time to analyze a situation, let your intuition and sense of humor be your guides. It is more important to change the direction of the energy than to find the perfect solution.
- You do not have to explain or talk about everything; keeping the energy going in positive directions is more important.

ACKNOWLEDGMENTS

This book would have been impossible without the author of *Education for Life*, J. Donald Walters, known also as Swami Kriyananda. I was inspired and guided by his ability to articulate the ancient wisdom of the *vedas* and principles of yoga that could be applied in all walks of modern life and compatible with all religions.

Bryan (Aryavan) McSweeny, your enthusiasm for Education for Life inspired me to revisit my manuscript and start writing again!

And, Erin Vinnaco, your ability to understand and communicate the eight keys helped me clarify and refine this text beyond what I thought was possible. Your encouragement kept me going this last year of finishing the book. Thank you for that—and the title!

Lorna Knox, you read so many versions of so much writing over the years, and your encouragement was vital. The energy flowed easily when we worked on our first books together, *I Came from Joy*, and *Calm and Compassionate Children*, plus the Joyful Path Sunday School curriculum.

Thank you to everyone else who has encouraged me, and especially the proofreaders. I am so grateful for all the parents and teachers who recognized that what we were doing was special and a step toward the ideals we all shared.

I thank **all** of the teachers who collaborated, learned, and grew with me in the Living Wisdom School in Portland. To name a few, David Eby and Matthew Fredrickson, you brought the music, commitment, and the male perspective the school needed.

Karen (Bharati) Busch and Helen Gorman were there from the very beginning and never wavered. Bharati's proofing of this book turned into so much fun editing and reminiscing. And Sandi Goodwin, Melanie Brenneis, Trina Gardner, Sonali Gupta, and Rose Neal—you all gave so generously of yourselves. To quote Sandi, "All of you are always in my heart."

Thank you, Narayan and Dharmadevi Romano and everyone at Crystal Clarity. And lastly, Jyotish and Devi Novak, I deeply feel and appreciate your friendship and guidance.

ABOUT THE AUTHOR

SUSAN USHA DERMOND, BA, MA, MLS, has a varied background in education, most of it in the Education for Life system. She began her career as an English teacher in public high schools and most recently taught high school English in the Ananda Online High School. She founded the third Living Wisdom School in Portland, Oregon, where she was the director for fifteen years, and prior to that, taught fourth through ninth grades at the first Living Wisdom School at Ananda Village in northern California, where she currently lives. She developed the first online Education for Life classes and is the author of a handbook for teachers and parents, *Calm and Compassionate Children* (Random House).

Further Explorations

Crystal Clarity Publishers

If you enjoyed this title, Crystal Clarity Publishers invites you to deepen your spiritual life through many additional resources based on the teachings of Paramhansa Yogananda. We offer books, e-books, and audiobooks, a wide variety of inspirational and relaxation music composed by Swami Kriyananda, and yoga and meditation videos.

See a listing of books below or visit our secure website for a complete online catalog, or to place an order for our products.

crystalclarity.com
800.424.1055 | clarity@crystalclarity.com
1123 Goodrich Blvd. | Commerce, CA 90022

Ananda Worldwide

Crystal Clarity Publishers is the publishing house of Ananda, a worldwide spiritual movement founded by Swami Kriyananda, a direct disciple of Paramhansa Yogananda. Ananda offers resources and support for your spiritual journey through meditation instruction, webinars, online virtual community, email, and chat.

Ananda has more than 150 centers and meditation groups in over forty-five countries, offering group-guided meditations, classes and teacher training in meditation and yoga, and many other resources.

In addition, Ananda has developed eight residential communities in the US, Europe, and India. Spiritual communities are places where people live together in a spirit of cooperation and friendship, dedicated to a common goal. Spirituality is practiced in all areas of daily life: at school, at work, or in the home. Many Ananda communities offer internships where one can stay and experience spiritual community firsthand.

For more information about Ananda communities or meditation groups near you, please visit **ananda.org** or call **530.478.7560**.

The Expanding Light Retreat

The Expanding Light is the largest retreat center in the world to share exclusively the teachings of Paramhansa Yogananda. Situated in the Ananda Village community near Nevada City, California, it offers the opportunity to experience spiritual life in a contemporary ashram setting. The varied, year-round schedule of classes and programs on yoga, meditation, and spiritual practice includes Karma Yoga, personal retreat, spiritual travel, and online learning. Large groups are welcome.

The Ananda School of Yoga & Meditation offers certified yoga, yoga therapist, spiritual counselor, and meditation teacher trainings.

The teaching staff has years of experience practicing Kriya Yoga meditation and all aspects of Paramhansa Yogananda's teachings. You may come for a relaxed personal renewal, participating in ongoing activities as much or as little as you wish. The serene mountain setting, supportive staff, and delicious vegetarian meals provide an ideal environment for a truly meaningful stay, be it a brief respite or an extended spiritual vacation.

For more information, please visit **expandinglight.org** or call **800.346.5350.**

Ananda Meditation Retreat

Set amidst seventy-two acres of beautiful meditation gardens and wild forest in Northern California's Sierra foothills, the Ananda Meditation Retreat is an ideal setting for a rejuvenating, inner experience.

The Meditation Retreat has been a place of deep meditation and sincere devotion for over fifty years. Long before that, the Native American Maidu tribe held this to be sacred land. The beauty and presence of the Divine are tangibly felt by all who come here.

Studies show that being in nature and using techniques such as forest bathing can significantly reduce stress and blood pressure while strengthening your immune system, concentration, and level of happiness. The Meditation Retreat is the perfect place for quiet immersion in nature.

Plan a personal retreat, enjoy one of the guided

retreats, or choose from a variety of programs led by the caring and joyful staff.

For more information or to place your reservation, please visit meditationretreat.org, call 530.478.7557, or email meditationretreat@ananda.org.

THE ORIGINAL WRITINGS OF PARAMHANSA YOGANANDA

1946 Unedited Edition of Paramhansa Yogananda's Spiritual Masterpiece

AUTOBIOGRAPHY OF A YOGI
Paramhansa Yogananda

Autobiography of a Yogi is one of the world's most acclaimed spiritual classics, with millions of copies sold. Named one of the Best 100 Spiritual Books of the twentieth century, this book helped launch and continues to inspire a spiritual awakening throughout the Western world.

Yogananda was the first yoga master of India whose mission brought him to live and teach in the West. His firsthand account of his life experiences in India includes childhood revelations, stories of his visits to saints and masters, and long-secret teachings of yoga and self-realization that he first made available to the Western reader.

This reprint of the original 1946 edition is free from textual changes made after Yogananda's passing in 1952. This updated edition includes bonus materials: the last chapter that Yogananda wrote in 1951, also without posthumous changes, the eulogy Yogananda wrote for Gandhi, and a new foreword and afterword by Swami Kriyananda, one of Yogananda's close, direct disciples.

Also available in Spanish and Hindi from Crystal Clarity Publishers

SCIENTIFIC HEALING AFFIRMATIONS
Paramhansa Yogananda

This reprint of the original 1924 classic by Paramhansa Yogananda is a pioneering work in the field of self-healing and self-transformation. He explains that words are crystallized thoughts and have life-changing power when spoken with conviction, concentration, willpower, and feeling. Yogananda offers far more than mere suggestions for achieving positive attitudes. He shows how to impregnate words with spiritual force to shift habitual thought patterns of the mind and create a new personal reality.

Added to this text are over fifty of Yogananda's well-loved "Short Affirmations," taken from issues of *East-West* and *Inner Culture* magazines from 1932 to 1942. This little book will be a treasured companion on the road to realizing your highest, divine potential.

METAPHYSICAL MEDITATIONS
Paramhansa Yogananda

Metaphysical Meditations is a classic collection of meditation techniques, visualizations, affirmations, and prayers from the great yoga master, Paramhansa Yogananda. The meditations given are of three types: those spoken to the individual consciousness, prayers or demands addressed to God, and affirmations that bring us closer to the Divine.

Select a passage that meets your specific need and speak each word slowly and purposefully until you become absorbed in its inner meaning. At the bedside, by the meditation seat, or while traveling—one can choose no better companion than *Metaphysical Meditations*.

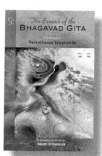

THE ESSENCE OF THE BHAGAVAD GITA
Explained by Paramhansa Yogananda
As remembered by his disciple, Swami Kriyananda

Rarely in a lifetime does a new spiritual classic appear that has the power to change people's lives and transform future generations. This is such a book. This revelation of India's best-loved scripture approaches it from a fresh perspective, showing its deep allegorical meaning and down-to-earth practicality. The themes presented are universal: how to achieve victory in life in union with the Divine; how to prepare for life's "final exam," death, and what happens afterward; and how to triumph over all pain and suffering.

The book itself is a triumph. Swami Kriyananda worked with Paramhansa Yogananda in 1950 while the Master completed his commentary. At that time, Yogananda commissioned him to disseminate his teachings worldwide.

"*Millions will find God through this book!*" Yogananda declared upon completion of the manuscript. "*Not just thousands—millions. I have seen it. I know.*"

EDUCATION FOR LIFE
Explained by Paramhansa Yogananda
J. Donald Walters

Education for Life offers a constructive and brilliant alternative to what has been called the disaster of modern education. The need for a change is universally recognized. In this book, Kriyananda traces the problems to an emphasis on technological competence at the expense of spiritual values, which alone can give higher meaning to life. *Education for Life* offers parents, educators, and concerned citizens everywhere techniques that are both compassionate and practical.

Based on the pioneering work in India of Paramhansa Yogananda, in the early twentieth century, this book offers a workable combination of idealism and practicality telling educators what to teach, when to teach it, how to teach it, and why. The Education for Life system has been tested and proven for over three decades at the many Living Wisdom schools located throughout the United States. Educators in both American and Europe have acclaimed the Living Wisdom schools as places where children are encouraged to grow toward full maturity as human beings, and where they learn not only facts, but also innovative principles for better living.

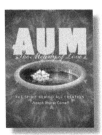

AUM: THE MELODY OF LOVE
Explained by Paramhansa Yogananda
Joseph Bharat Cornell

We have all heard of the sacred word *AUM*, and heard it chanted as a mantra by meditators. But what is *AUM*, and what does it signify? This book takes readers on a journey into the deeper teachings of *AUM*, and the blissful realizations that await those who access this expansive sound vibration.

Seek the sound that never ceases. The winds of God's grace constantly flow into this world through Holy *AUM*. The Sacred Sound has many names, and mystics of all religions revere it. Just as light is intrinsic to a lighted lamp, the sound of *AUM* is integral to the presence of Spirit. God's nature is bliss, and to share His joy, He created the universe through Cosmic Vibration. The sound of the Cosmic Vibration is *AUM*, and listening to it brings the greatest bliss imaginable. *AUM* is the Omnipotent Force that propels each soul toward Spirit. It is the sacred, inner fire. As you approach the cosmic blaze, you feel at first its radiant, soothing comfort; then, as you come closer—*AUM* liberating flames consume you—and bring you to God.

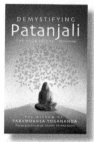

DEMYSTIFYING PATANJALI: THE YOGA SUTRAS
The Wisdom of Paramhansa Yogananda
Presented by his direct disciple, Swami Kriyananda

Demystifying Patanjali represents the confluence of three great yoga teachers. Patanjali, the first exponent of the ancient teachings of yoga, presented his system of inner contemplation, meditation practice, and ethics. Paramhansa Yogananda, perhaps the greatest of all yoga masters to live and teach in the West, revealed with deep insight the meaning behind Patanjali's often obscure aphorisms. Finally, Yogananda's direct disciple, Swami Kriyananda, the author of nearly 150 spiritual books in his own right, compiled his guru's explanation into a clear, systematic presentation.

These three great souls combine to give us a modern scripture that will enlighten the mind, expand the heart, and inspire the soul of every seeker.

·